"T

Lady Milbanke, widow of the famous Diplomat, has a fantastic soprano voice, but she was never of course, allowed to sing in public.

However, after she was widowed she and her daughter Carla were so poor they were on the verge of starvation.

Unexpectedly she meets again the famous impresario Gustav Dessoff who knew her when she lived in Italy, because she was half Italian.

He begs her to sing in Opera and because she is so worried about her daughter she agrees to do so.

They go to Vienna and Carla is told on no account must she use her own name or be her mother's daughter, but must travel as a friend and a companion.

In Vienna they first of all meet the Baron Otto von Erhardt to whom Carla takes a great dislike as he appears very familiar.

She also encounters in the Opera House a young man who says his name is Rákóczi and she tells him shyly her name is Carla.

Because he realizes what she wants more than anything else, he takes her to The Spanish Riding School, in secret, to see the Empress Elizabeth ride with the famous horses.

As one of his horses is appearing in the Opera "Die Walküre" they meet again in the Opera House and Rákóczi learns that Carla longs to hear Johann Strauss play his magical music.

He arranges this when Lady Milbanke, under her assumed name, is singing in the Palace to the Emperor.

Then he confesses to Carla that he is in fact Prince Rákóczi, the descendent of the famous hero of Hungary.

He tells her that because she is a commoner he cannot marry her and he is therefore saying good-bye although he loves her with all his heart.

He leaves her in tears, but when she goes into her bedroom she finds Baron Otto von Erhardt waiting for her.

How the Prince saves her from the Baron and how he realizes nothing is more important than love is told in this romantic 432nd story by Barbara Cartland.

Barbara Cartland's most recent books:

Pan Books	*The Necklace of Love* *The Taming of a Tigress* *Love at First Sight* *Paradise in Penang* *Solita and the Spies* *A Knight in Paris* *The Lady and the Highwayman* *The Passionate Princess* *Revenge is Sweet* *The Chieftain Finds Love* *The Lovely Liar* *The Temple of Love* *A Revolution of Love* *A Hazard of Hearts*
New English Library	*The Perfect Pearl* *The Perfume of the Gods* *Never Forget Love*
Severn House	*A Game of Love* *Love Casts out Fear* *Imperial Splendour* *Conquered by Love* *The Curse of the Clan* *Lovers in Paradise*
Robert Hale	*A Nightingale Sang* *The Saint and the Sinner* *Love in the Clouds* *Punishment of a Vixen*

"THE MUSIC OF LOVE"

BY

BARBARA CARTLAND

THE MUSIC OF LOVE

A T.C.C.L. Book ISBN 1 872113 04 4

First publication in Great Britain

T.C.C.L. edition published 1989

T.C.C.L. books are published by
The Communication Circle Limited
9–10 Bentinck Mews
London
W1M 5FL

Typeset, printed and bound in Great Britain by
Hazell Watson & Viney Limited
Member of BPCC Limited
Aylesbury, Bucks, England

AUTHOR'S NOTE

I first visited Vienna in 1933 with my brother Ronald Cartland who was later to be the first Member of Parliament to be killed in the War.

We were tremendously impressed by the Stefanstock and I had a strange vision of a Cardinal when I was in it.

The second time I went to Vienna was in 1969, when the Mayor gave me a Civic Reception for my work for Health.

The third time was last year – 1986, when I was promoting my books in Germany and was also having a film taken of my life.

I had the great joy of going into The Spanish Riding School with the Director. I was filmed patting one of the horses and talking to the rider.

I also appeared on the stage of the magnificent Opera House and mimed to one of the Love Songs on my album which I had previously made with The Royal Philharmonic Orchestra.

Later I was interviewed in the Royal Box and it was a tremendous experience to see the marvellous building both from the audience and from the stage.

On each of these three visits I stayed at the wonderful Hôtel Sacher, and not only eat the delicious, world-famous Sacher Cake, but went down to the Kitchens to see it being made.

Vienna will always be one of the most romantic and fascinating Cities in the world.

When I wrote "The Private Life of Elizabeth, Empress of Austria", I was so very touched to learn from Earl Mountbatten of Burma that it was appreciated by the Elizabeth Club who said it was one of the best biographies that had ever been written about her.

Vienna is not only a City of music, but to me a City of love.

CHAPTER ONE

1877

Lady Milbanke looked up from her desk as her daughter Carla came into the room.

"It is no use, Mama," Carla said. "I went with Bessie to price the chickens, but they are much too expensive for us to afford one!"

For a moment Lady Milbanke did not answer.

She was thinking how lovely her daughter looked.

The cold air outside had brought a flush to her cheeks, and her small pointed face was framed by the woollen hood she wore.

Lady Milbanke was thinking that other girls of Carla's age would be wearing a hood trimmed with fur.

Instead of which she was painfully aware that Carla's coat was too small for her, and anyway it was threadbare.

". . .so we bought some scraps of meat instead," Carla was saying, "for Bessie to make a stew."

She wrinkled her small nose.

"I am tired of stew, and I know you are too, Mama, but honestly, there was nothing else we could afford."

Lady Milbanke sighed.

It was a deep sigh that seemed to come from the very depths of her thin body.

At thirty-eight she was still very beautiful.

Like her daughter, if she could have afforded to be fashionably dressed, she would have looked a sensation at any of the parties to which they were no longer invited.

Ever since Lord Milbanke had died a year ago they had begun to fall out of the fashionable world in which he had moved simply because they could not afford it.

It was not only gowns which were far beyond the reach of Lady Milbanke's purse.

As she could not return hospitality, she was too proud to accept it.

Now, as she looked at her daughter, she wondered if in fact, she should have tried to inveigle invitations for Carla if not for herself.

She had been so miserable when her husband died unexpectedly.

Although he was some years older than she was, they were very happy.

When she realised the financial situation in which she had been left, she first felt helpless.

She could not bear the sympathy of people who, in the past, had fawned on her husband.

Not only because he was important diplomatically, but also because he was a clever and interesting man.

It was quite a different thing for hostesses to entertain a widow with a daughter who was a rival to their own children.

What was more, Lady Milbanke could barely afford a hired carriage to take them out to dinner.

"How could Papa's affairs be in such a mess?" Carla had asked despairingly.

Her mother had just explained that they actually had nothing to live on, and she replied:

"Your father was never a good business man. He had a large salary in the Diplomatic Service and he spent every penny of it! The money he inherited from his father was badly invested."

She felt tears come into her eyes as she remembered how the Solicitors, after Lord Milbanke's death, had read her his assets.

They had made it quite clear that everything in which he had invested his money had been a disaster.

It had been a case of bankrupt firms and financiers who had absconded with their clients' money.

Also 'flash-in-the-pan', and 'get-rich-quick' ideas which were always failures.

It meant that Lord Milbanke's widow was left but a house that nobody wanted to buy, and which contained very little to sell.

She had sold what she could, month by month, week by week.

Now she knew that, unless they were to starve, she must find something else.

Because Lady Milbanke shrank from going herself to the Pawn Brokers' shops, she left the negotiations to Bessie.

She was their only remaining servant, an old maid who had been with them for ten years.

She often thought, however, that Bessie was not particularly clever at negotiating a good price.

'I will go myself,' she decided, and wondered what with.

Carla walked round the desk and put her arm round her mother.

"You are looking sad, Mama," she said, "and you know Papa liked you to smile and look happy."

"It is difficult," Lady Milbanke murmured, with a little break in her voice.

"Come and sing for me," Carla begged, "as you used to sing to Papa."

Lady Milbanke gave an unexpected laugh.

"At this time of the morning?"

"What does it matter what time it is?" Carla asked. "When I hear you singing I feel as if I am carried into another world where there are no worries, no troubles. I am sure that is what Papa used to feel."

Lady Milbanke rose from the desk.

"I suppose, really," she said, "I ought to sell the piano."

Carla gave a cry of horror.

"Oh, no, Mama! How could you think of doing such a thing? You know how much it means to you – and to me!"

Lady Milbanke crossed the room to sit down at the grand piano which stood in an alcove at the end of it.

It was true she had an unusually beautiful voice.

Her husband had made her sing to him most evenings when they were alone.

They had therefore arranged the piano so that he could watch her comfortably from his arm-chair.

It was raised a little on a small platform.

He had made the background for her, while somewhat theatrical, very beautiful.

Unfortunately now that they needed the money, they could not sell the murals of flowers and birds against which the piano stood.

It had cost Lord Milbanke a great deal of money to have them painted exactly to his liking.

Lady Milbanke sat down on the piano-stool, her dark hair silhouetted against the sunshine in which flew exotic birds.

Beneath them there were flowers of every colour, stretching away into a misty horizon.

Lady Milbanke ran her fingers over the keys.

The she started to sing very softly an Italian song which she knew was one of her daughter's favourites.

There was no doubt her voice was outstanding.

As she sang she forgot her troubles and it seemed to Carla as if her mother was an angel singing in the sky.

Her voice echoed and re-echoed round the Drawing-Room.

Only when the song ended and Lady Milbanke let her

hands fall into her lap did Carla realise she had been listening almost breathlessly.

"That was wonderful, Mama!" she said. "I have never heard you sing better!"

Lady Milbanke put out her hand to touch the piano as if she was caressing it.

"Your father paid a great deal of money for this," she said wistfully.

"You are not to sell it, Mama," Carla protested jumping out of the chair in which she had been sitting.

"It will not be much use to us if we have nothing to eat!" her mother pointed out.

Carla leaned on the piano.

"Are things really as bad as that?"

"I am afraid they are desperate!" Lady Milbanke said, "I must pay Bessie's wages. She has had nothing for three months!"

"Perhaps," Carla said hesitatingly, "we could . . approach one of . . Papa's relatives and . . ask them to help us."

"How can we possibly do that?" Lady Milbanke asked quickly. "They have never been to see us since your father died. Anyway, none of them are rich. In fact, they consider themselves to be very poor!"

"Then I must find something to do," Carla said. "Surely after the very expensive and extensive education I have had, I could earn some money, even if it is only as a Governess?"

Her mother laughed.

"Darling, I cannot imagine anybody employing you as a Governess!"

"Why not?" Carla asked.

"Because, my dearest, you are far too pretty – and pretty Governesses are notorious trouble-makers in any family. If she is only eighteen and looks like a Spring flower, then a Lady, unless she is blind, would not allow her to cross her threshold!"

Carla laughed.

"You sound exactly like one of those novels you do not approve of me reading!"

Her mother shrugged her shoulders.

Carla thought with a smile, although she did not say so, that at times her mother's Italian blood was very obvious.

Lady Milbanke was in fact only half-Italian, the daughter of the *Conte di Ravello* and his English wife.

There was no doubt that it was her Italian background that had given her such a beautiful voice.

Also the dark eyes that seemed to shine when she was happy, and flash fire when she was angry.

At the same time, her English mother was responsible for the white skin and the clear-cut classical features which her daughter had inherited.

Carla, however, was more like her father than her mother.

Her fair hair with touches of gold in it resembled the pictures of her father's ancestors.

Unfortunately, the beautiful Lady Milbanke had not been painted by the famous artists of their day, which would have made the pictures more saleable.

Lady Milbanke walked across the room.

As she reached her desk Carla knew that once again her Mother was aware of how little money they had.

She was in fact, wondering what else they could sell.

The jewels which Lord Milbanke had given his lovely wife had been the first to be sold.

They paid for the Funeral and the more pressing of his creditors.

Then their furs had gone.

The chinchilla cape which Lady Milbanke had worn

to the Opera, the sable tie and muff which had been the envy of her friends.

The ermine wrap, which made the plainest evening gown look elegant, followed.

After them had gone the silver which had fetched very little.

The china ornaments had fetched even less.

As had any other objects which Bessie could dispose of amongst the junk shops in Islington.

Lord Milbanke had bought a house there when it was still a popular area.

Although not so fashionable as it had been at the beginning of Queen Victoria's reign.

He had decided when he saw the house, that it was a bargain, considering its size.

He wanted somewhere he could entertain when he was in London.

He thought vaguely when he retired from the Diplomatic Service he would then buy a place in the country.

He had always lived in grandour.

Owing to the various posts he had held he had been provided with a house and servants, carriages and horses.

He had never really questioned whether or not he could afford it.

It was when he was at the Embassy in Rome that he had fallen head-over-heels in love for the first time in his life.

He was thirty-eight, and although he had enjoyed a great number of love affairs, he had never met anyone he wanted to marry.

When he first saw Maria, the seventeen-year-old daughter of the *Conte di Ravello* he knew he could not live without her.

She was not only beautiful, but she captivated him with her lovely voice.

Lord Milbanke had always been musical.

As he had worked in the Embassies of Budapest, Vienna, St. Petersburg, then Rome, music was very much a part of his life.

When he had heard Maria sing, he felt that he was hearing for the first time the voice of an angel.

It was in fact quite by chance they met at a party given especially for the King of Italy.

Lord Milbanke, although not yet an Ambassador was, through sheer brilliance, of diplomatic importance.

After a long-drawn-out and very elaborate dinner the guests had repaired to the Salon.

They were told they would hear music and songs which had been specially arranged by Gustav Dessoff from Vienna.

As Lord Milbanke knew, Gustav Dessoff had already made his mark in the Music World.

He remembered meeting him on several occasions.

He was an Austrian belonging to a good family who, however, was not content to stay on his comfortable estate in the country.

Instead he devoted himself to the development of music.

He specialised in finding musicians and singers who, under his patronage, became acknowledged stars.

It so happened that Dessoff was in Rome at the time of the party.

He was invited to bring for His Majesty's entertainment some of his discoveries to perform after dinner.

As usual, Dessoff was looking for something new.

He was sure the King would be well acquainted with the Principals of the Operas.

He wondered whether he could find somebody different to provide, if nothing else, a talking point in the evening.

He was considered whether it would be worth sending

to Paris for a Baritone he had just discovered and whom he thought was exceptional.

Or alternatively he should ask a Soprano he had heard in Milan to come to Rome.

Then his Cousin with whom he was staying insisted he should attend a Concert at a nearby Seminary for Young Ladies.

She told him her daughter was to play the piano.

Gustav Dessoff thought that nothing would bore him more.

Yet because he was a kind man he agreed.

He thought it would be a wasted afternoon when he might be tasting the joys of Rome.

As he expected, the Concert was held in the Assembly Hall of the School.

The girls came on to the platform one after another, to show their parents what their music Teacher had taught them.

She was an elderly woman with no talent of her own.

Gustav Dessoff sat praying that the Concert would end quickly so that he could escape.

Then a girl appeared who he thought was at least, extremely pretty.

Certainly she stood out amongst the other pupils like a jewel in a rough setting.

When she began to sing Gustav Dessoff caught his breath.

At the first notes he knew that she was exceptional, and by the time she had finished he was ecstatic.

Never, he thought, had he heard a lovelier voice that was so pure.

With her top notes Maria seemed to touch the sky.

He could hardly wait until the Concert was over when he might be introduced to the girl who had sung like an angel.

He learned that her name was Maria Ravello, and that her mother, the *Contessa* was in the audience.

Gustav Dessoff found no difficulty in getting himself invited to the *Conte's* home.

There Maria sang to him again.

He knew he was not mistaken in thinking she was one of the exceptional people born with a perfect voice that hardly needed training.

He tried to explain to the *Conte* and his wife how unusual their daughter was.

They were pleased at his appreciation.

Because he was so persausive, they allowed Maria to sing at the party which was being given for the King.

"I trust," the *Contessa* said in her quiet English voice, "that the other performers are known to you? Otherwise it would be a mistake for Maria to mix with them."

Gustav Dessoff understood exactly what she was saying.

He promised that Maria would be carefully chaperoned and protected but not only from the performers.

He was thinking that some of the guests might think that because she was with him they might be familiar with her.

The *Contessa* was obviously anxious about her lovely daughter, which was understandable.

Gustav Dessoff however succeeded in having them invited to the party after the dinner.

This was a concession which the *Conte* appreciated.

He knew that in no other circumstances would he have been fortunate enough to have been included in such a special Royal party.

Maria sang.

Once she had started she was not nervous because as usual, the music carried her away into another world.

She had not the slightest idea how lovely she looked

standing on the small stage which was massed with flowers.

It had been erected at the end of the Salon for the performance.

With Maria in mind, Gustav Dessoff had arranged that the rest of the music was very different.

There was a Pianist who was world famous, a Violinist who came from Hungary, and a Quartet that was good enough to please the most critical Italians.

But there was only one singer, and that was Maria.

He had asked if she could wear a white gown, and she looked like a lily with her dark hair and white skin.

When she had finished singing there was that pregnant silence which every professional knows is the greatest compliment they can receive.

Then the applause was, for such a distinguished company, ecstatic.

Gustav Dessoff had afterwards begged the *Conte* and *Contessa* to let him take Maria under his wing.

"I will produce her," he said, "at all the great Opera Houses in Europe."

Because he was so insistent they were finding it hard to refuse him when Lord Milbanke appeared on the scene.

He had been at the Concert, heard Maria sing, and lost his heart.

They were married a month later.

"You will never again appear in public, my darling," he said, "and only sing for me, but I promise you will never have a more appreciative audience."

He was handsome, experienced and very gentle with her.

Maria fell in love and was willing to do anything he suggested.

"I shall never forget you," Gustav Dessoff said when he came to her wedding.

He gave her a very expensive present.

"Sometimes, when you look at this," he had said, "remember that to me you were the treasure that was out of reach, the dream that never came true!"

She had smiled and thought she would forget him.

She travelled with her husband to different countries and listened to many singers.

Sometimes she thought a little wistfully that she might have sung 'Carmen' or 'Aida'.

She knew that she would have been better than many of the Principals taking a leading part.

Lord Milbanke had never allowed her to sing for anyone but himself and their daughter Carla.

Once when she had suggested that she might sing to their friends who were coming to dinner, he had replied angrily:

"Do you think I want my wife looked at as if she was an actress? Your voice is mine, and no other man shall hear it!"

He had kissed her fiercely and possessively and she knew that he was very jealous.

She loved him because he was dominating and her whole life revolved around him.

When he died there was nothing.

Only an emptiness and the ceaseless worry about money for which she had no solution.

"If I had a voice like yours, Mama," Carla was saying now, "I am sure people would pay me to sing, even if it was only in the street!"

Lady Milbanke laughed.

"I am afraid, my darling, while you have many talents, singing is not one of them."

"I know that," Carla said, "but my talents do not seem to be very saleable."

"We must sell something," Lady Milbanke said desperately, "but I cannot think what."

Bessie came into the room at that moment.

"Luncheon's ready, M'Lady," she announced, " 'though, if yer asks me, 'tis not enough t'keep a mouse alive!"

"I know, Bessie," Lady Milbanke said. "Miss Carla was telling me how everything was too expensive this morning."

"We can't go on like this, an' that's a fact!" Bessie said.

"I know," Lady Milbanke agreed walking towards the door.

Carla followed her and Bessie came behind them.

"I 'eard you singin'," Bessie said as she shuffled along. "It's a pity you can't enter for t'competition they're 'avin' at Covent Garden."

"What competition is that?" Carla asked.

"Me niece was talkin' about it when I visits 'er yesterday," Bessie replied. "Seems some ol' Josser 'as come to London and wants t'find a new star t'sing in Vena or some such place!"

They reached the Dining-Room and Lady Milbanke sat down at the table with Carla beside her.

On the table, Bessie had put a china bowl containing a small amount of meat stew.

She had added two or three carrots and an onion which she and Carla had bought in the market.

It was a dish they had regularly, simply because it was the cheapest they could buy.

Bessie went back to the Kitchen to fetch the plates she had left to warm on the stove.

She put them down in front of Lady Milbanke, saying as she did so:

"Me niece can dance, an' as yer knows, hers been in the chorus at Covent Garden fer three years, but she's got a voice like a crow!"

She laughed at her own joke.

Then as Carla realised her mother was taking no interest in what Bessie was saying, she asked:

"Are there many girls entering the competition?"

"No, only two or three who've been told they 'as a chance. This Austrian or whatever 'e is, is ever so partic'lar but they says that if 'e finds someun 'e fancies 'e can make 'em thousands of pounds!"

There was a note of envy in Bessie's voice and Carla laughed.

"Well, I was just saying to Mama that I will never make a fortune by singing."

She looked at her mother and said:

"That is true, Mama, is it not, and I do not think I would be much use as a dancer."

Lady Milbanke was ladling the largest portion of the stew on to a plate for her daughter.

As if she was suddenly aware of what was being said she asked:

"Who is this man who is judging the girls? Did your niece tell you his name?"

"Her did, but I can't remember it," Bessie replied. "Now let I think – it was very outlandish – Dress – off – or somethin' like that."

Lady Milbanke put down the spoon.

"Was it by any chance 'Gustav Dessoff'?" she asked.

"Yeah, that's it!" Bessie replied. "I can't think 'ow them foreigners can remember their names!"

She walked out of the Dining-Room as she spoke.

"Gustav Dessoff!" Lady Milbanke said softly.

"Have you heard of him, Mama?" Carla asked.

She was eating quickly what was on her plate because she was very hungry.

"I knew him in the past," Lady Milbanke replied. "He thought my voice was exceptional."

"Which it is!"

Carla looked up.

"Mama! You are not thinking of going in for the competition!"

She was joking, but her mother did not answer.

"Are you?"

There was a long pause before her mother said:

"I am going to Covent Garden this afternoon to see Gustav Dessoff again."

. . . .

It was evening before Lady Milbanke returned to the house in Islington.

When she had left, dressed in the best clothes they had between them, Carla thought she looked very pretty.

"Do take me with you, Mama," she pleaded.

Her mother shook her head.

"No, Carla. I have no wish for you to go inside the Theatre, or to have anything to do with the theatrical profession. It is something of which your father would not have approved."

"But you are going there, Mama!"

"I am going to see an old friend, and very likely he has forgotten all about me," Lady Milbanke answered. "But there is a chance, just a chance, Carla, that he might be able to help us."

Then she added in a low voice as if she spoke to herself:

"After all, I have nothing to lose by trying."

"How are you going to get to Covent Garden, Mama?" Carla asked. "It is a long way."

"I shall have to take a cab," Lady Milbanke replied.

She looked round helplessly as if for inspiration, then drew off her wedding ring.

"Ask Bessie to run round to the Pawnbroker's with this."

"But . . Mama . . it is your Wedding ring . . you cannot sell that!"

"We can sell something else and buy it back, but I cannot waste time looking now."

She had a feeling that Gustav Dessoff would not spend very much time in England.

If he found what he wanted at Covent Garden he would leave at once.

If he did not, there would be no point in him staying.

Bessie, grumbling because she had already been out once today, went off to the Pawnbroker, whose shop was only two streets away.

She came back with very little money.

"I says as 'ow you'd be in to claim it, M'Lady, but 'e said weddin' rings be 'two a penny' round 'ere."

Lady Milbanke looked at the money Bessie handed her.

"This will get me to Covent Garden," she said. "In case I have to walk home do not worry if I am late."

"Oh, Mama, you ought not to go alone," Carla said. "Please, let me come with you."

"No, darling, it would be a mistake," Lady Milbanke said.

Carla walked with her until they found a Hackney Cab, helped her into it and told the Cabby where to go.

She thought he sniffed as he drove off.

'I suppose,' she thought as she walked home, 'Papa would be shocked at Mama going to the Stage-Door of a Theatre. At the same time if Mr. Dessoff is rich enough to give us a good dinner, I shall be grateful."

Because she was still hungry, as she walked home, she was thinking what dishes she would choose.

That was, if money was no object and somebody else was paying for the meal.

She reached the house and went to the Kitchen.

In the past, when her father had been alive, there had been a Cook and two scullions to prepare their meals.

Now there was only Bessie, drinking a cup of tea.

"Yer got yer mother off, Miss Carla?" she asked.

"Yes, and I hope she will be all right," Carla replied, sitting down on one of the kitchen chairs.

"That's more than we are!" Bessie said, "an' now I thinks o' it, I should 'ave kept some o' that money from 'Er Ladyship's ring to buy some tatties, if nothin' else, fer supper."

"I am tired of potatoes, scraps of stale bread and stew!" Carla murmured.

"Yer'll 'ave t' make yer mother do somethin' about it," Bessie remarked. "Surely someun would make an offer fer this 'ouse?"

"We have put it in the hands of three different Agents," Carla said, "but they say it is too big, and the people who live in this area want something smaller."

She sighed.

"Papa always liked everything big, grand and opulent!"

"So should I, if I 'ad the chance!" Bessie said.

Because the way she spoke was so funny, Carla laughed.

"There is only one thing we can do, Bessie, and that is to pray that by some miraculous way Mama will come back with a bag of gold!"

"That's as likely as Father Christmas droppin' down th' Chimley with a turkey fer us!" Bessie replied tartly.

"I could eat two, and still feel hungry!" Carla said wistfully.

When she was tired of talking to Bessie, she went into the Dining-Room.

She wondered, as she had wondered a hundred times before, what she could do to earn a little money.

'There must be something I can do,' she thought.

'Even if I was a shop-girl or a crossing-sweeper it would be better than just starving to death!'

The hours seemed to drag by slowly.

When it was six o'clock, she was beginning to think frantically that something had happened to her mother.

Then she heard the sound of horses' hoofs outside and ran quickly to open the front door.

She was expecting to see her mother get out of the same sort of dingy cab with a tired horse in which she had set off for Covent Garden.

To her surprise, however, there was an expensive-looking carriage outside, drawn by two horses.

The coachman, wearing a cockaded hat, was sitting on the box while a foot man had climbed down to open the carriage door.

Her mother got out and one glance at her told Carla that her eyes were shining, and she was excited.

"You are back, Mama!" she exclaimed.

Then as she ran to kiss her she saw that her mother was not alone.

A man was stepping out of the carriage after her and she knew without being told that this was Gustav Dessoff.

"Yes, I am back!" Lady Milbanke said, "And I have brought an old friend to meet you, darling."

They went into the house.

As Gustav Dessoff took off his tall hat and fur-lined coat in the hall Carla thought that he looked rich and prosperous.

She was sure her mother had brought back good news.

They went into the Drawing-Room before Lady Milbanke said:

"I want to introduce you to my daughter Carla. She is, as you see, not in the least like I was when we first met."

"But very beautiful," Gustav Dessoff said.

He had a deep voice with a slight accent.

Carla thought that his eyes under his heavy eye-brows were shrewd and penetrating, while at the same time kind.

"Please sit down," Lady Milbanke said. "I am afraid . . although it seems very inhospitable . . that I have nothing to offer you to drink."

She spoke a little hesitatingly as if she was embarrassed, but Gustav Dessoff said:

"I want nothing but to look at you, Maria, and realise that you are just as beautiful, if not more so, than when I last saw you, on your wedding day!"

Lady Milbanke blushed.

"I wish that was true, but do you realise that Carla is a year older than I was when I married?"

"She, too, is very lovely!" Gustav Dessoff said gallantly, "but has she inherited your voice?"

"When I sing," Carla said before her mother could reply, "dogs howl, and the birds fly away!"

Gustav Dessoff laughed.

"That is certainly a tragedy! But now I want to hear your mother sing. I cannot believe her voice has been lost."

"No, of course not," Carla said quickly, "and Mama has sung for Papa and me, and it is the most beautiful sound I have ever heard!"

"That is what I want to make sure of," Gustav Dessoff said.

He looked at Lady Milbanke and said gently:

"Because I want to take you both out to dinner, are you too tired to sing for me now?"

"No, of course not," she answered, "Only afraid you will be disappointed."

"I have the feeling I shall not be. At the same time, you know me well enough to be aware that I shall tell you the truth!"

"That is what I want to hear," Lady Milbanke said.

She took off the coat she was wearing over her thin gown and also her hat.

As she did so, Gustav Dessoff went to the piano.

He sat down and struck a few chords and Carla knew without him saying anything that he was thinking the piano needed tuning.

Then as Lady Milbanke stepped on to the small platform, she asked:

"What would you like me to sing?"

"Anything you like," he replied.

"The aria from 'Carmen'," she suggested.

Without replying, he began to play very softly.

Carla sat down in a chair.

She was watching her mother, feeling that what was happening was something very important and that it would change their lives.

She was not certain how it would do so.

She only knew perceptively that her prayers had been answered in a very unexpected manner.

Then, as her mother began to sing, she could think of nothing but the beauty of her voice.

CHAPTER TWO

Carla woke in the morning feeling better and more alert than she had for a long time.

She knew it was due to the delicious dinner they had had last night with Gustav Dessoff.

He had taken them to a quiet Restaurant which was very luxurious and obviously very expensive.

Carla, looking at her mother, knew it was reminding her of the old days with her father, when they ate at all the best places wherever they were.

But Lady Milbanke was not allowed to look wistful for long.

Gustav Dessoff began to entertain her with witty, amusing anecdotes of his life since they had last met.

There was champagne to drink which Carla thought sparkled like the conversation.

She enjoyed herself more than she had done for a very long time.

When her father had been alive there had always been interesting and intelligent guests sitting round the table.

Although she was only occasionally allowed to come down to dinner, she was always at the luncheon parties.

There were Royal Princes, Statesmen, Politicians and Ambassadors who paid her mother compliments while listening to what her father had to say.

When he died she knew she had not only lost him, but the elegance and luxury with which he had surrounded himself.

Now with her mother laughing and looking extremely pretty she felt they had stepped back into the past.

She prayed that they could stay there.

When her mother had finished singing Gustav Dessoff had not spoken.

He had just sat for several seconds looking at her before her rose, and walking to her side raised her hand to his lips.

"Thank you," he said, "I knew that you would not disappoint me!"

Then he had left them to change their clothes for dinner and returned later to take them to the West End.

It might have been a struggle to find something decent to wear.

But the evening gowns Lady Milbanke had worn before her husband's death were still hanging in her wardrobe.

This was because they were unsaleable.

They were far too grand for the local people who had not the occasion to wear them.

They would buy anything serviceable.

But they just laughed at the idea of owning a gown which had been designed in Paris by Frederick Worth.

Lady Milbanke's dresses were all made of silk or satin, lace or tulle, and sparkled with diamanté.

Carla, wearing one of her mother's more simple gowns, and Lady Milbanke resplendent in one of the more elaborate looked, as Bessie described them, like Princesses.

"It's Buckin'am Palace ye should be orf to," she said, "and a King kissin' yer 'and, not that 'ere foreigner!"

Lady Milbanke laughed before she said:

"That 'Foreigner' as you describe him is, in his way, a King, and in fact the whole Music World bows down to him!"

"Well, let's 'ope 'e acts like one!" Bessie, who always had to have the last word, replied.

She waved to them as they drove away.

Carla looking at the light in her mother's eyes, thought she had never seen her look more lovely.

She knew there was one thing missing in their Fairy Tale and was sure her mother was conscious of it too.

Neither of them had any jewellery to wear.

There had been no time to redeem Lady Milbanke's wedding ring from the Pawnbroker's.

Carla was afraid that when her mother removed her gloves to eat, she would feel embarrassed.

Fortunately Gustav Dessoff prevented her from feeling anything but amused.

He had ordered the dinner before they arrived and for Carla every dish had been one she really enjoyed.

She had the feeling, however, that her mother was too intent on listening to her old friend to notice what she was eating.

At the same time, she was aware that they would both sleep well and feel better in the morning.

When they got back to the house, Gustav Dessoff helped them out of the carriage.

"Will you come in?" Lady Milbanke asked.

He shook his head.

"I want you to have a good night's rest," he replied, "and be ready to talk seriously to me in the morning. I will call on you at eleven o'clock."

He kissed her hand, and as she went in through the door, he returned to his carraige.

In the hall where, for economy's sake, there was only one candle burning, Lady Milbanke looked at her daughter.

"I am too tired to talk," she said before Carla could speak, "so we will both go to bed."

She picked up the candle as she spoke and carried it

up the stairs, holding up the skirt of her gown with her other hand.

Carla had gone to her bedroom with her.

"Let me unbutton your gown, Mama," she offered, "I am sure you cannot manage it yourself."

"Thank you, darling," Lady Milbanke replied, "and I will undo yours."

Carla was longing to ask why Gustav Dessoff was calling tomorrow morning.

But she was aware that her mother had, in some strange way, withdrawn into herself.

Then as she slipped off her gown, Lady Milbanke looked up at the picture that was above her bed.

It was one which had always been there, and because it was so beautifully painted, Carla was sure it would be saleable.

But she knew it meant a great deal to her mother.

It was a picture of the Virgin and Child, which Lady Milbanke looked at when she said her prayers.

Now as she glanced at it, Carla was perceptively aware that her mother was already praying about something very important.

She did not know what it was.

She was only certain that it was a problem over which she must ask God's guidance.

"Goodnight, Mama," she said softly, "it was a lovely evening and tomorrow, when Mr. Dessoff comes I will thank him."

"We must both do that," Lady Milbanke agreed.

She spoke in an absent-minded way, as if she was thinking of something else.

As Carla reached the door she glanced back to see her mother looking at the holy picture.

Because they had been out late Bessie did not wake them as early as usual.

There was certainly no reason to hurry down to breakfast.

It consisted only of some stale bread which Bessie had toasted, a small pot of not very fresh butter and some weak tea.

'Gustav Dessoff might ask us out to luncheon,' Carla thought hopefully.

When her mother came downstairs to her surprise she looked tired.

There were faint lines under her lovely eyes that were not usually there.

"Did you not sleep, Mama?" she asked.

"I had a lot to keep me awake," Lady Milbanke replied.

She did not explain and because Carla knew she did not wish to be questioned, she talked of other things.

The hours seemed to go slowly by until eleven o'clock.

They were both in the Drawing-Room when there was the rat-tat of the knocker on the front door.

Carla was aware that her mother started, clasped her hand together and looked pale.

"I expect that it is Mr. Dessoff," Carla said. "I will go and let him in."

Her mother did not speak and she hurried into the hall.

When she opened the door, Mr. Dessoff walked in.

Carla thought he looked even more impressive and prosperous than he had last night.

He was wearing his fur-lined coat, and there was a bunch of violets in his buttonhole.

He also carried a large bouquet of orchids which he gave to Carla saying:

"This is for your mother, and I have some other things in the carriage which will be carried into the kitchen."

Carla's eyes widened.

She saw a footman behind him carrying a large hamper.

On top of it was an open box in which there were half-a-dozen bottles of champagne.

Mr. Dessoff walked unannounced into the Drawing-Room and Carla led the footman into the Kitchen.

Bessie was there, and when she opened the hamper she exclaimed:

"Now that's wot I calls food!"

Mr. Dessoff had been very generous.

There were young chickens and a leg of lamb, a large pâté and a pot of caviar.

Various other pots and packages contained what Carla knew had been to them unobtainable luxuries.

She wanted to tell her mother about it right away and ran to the Drawing-Room.

As she opened the door she heard her mother say in a rather frightened voice:

"Are you . . certain I am . . doing the . . right thing?"

"I think, my dear," Mr. Dessoff replied quietly, "you have no alternative."

Because Carla felt they would not wish to be interrupted, she closed the door quietly and walked away.

At the same time, she was wondering frantically what it was her mother had promised to do.

She was certain that whatever it was, it could not be as bad as continuing to stay as they were and slowly starving to death.

Her mother and Gustav Dessoff were in the Drawing-Room for a long time.

Then at last, when she felt the suspense was almost unbearable, Carla heard her mother call her.

She ran from the Study where she had been walking restlessly up and down.

When she reached the Drawing-Room her mother said:

"Mr. Dessoff is taking us out to luncheon, so we will put on our bonnets quickly. We must not keep him waiting."

They went upstairs, Carla bursting with curiosity.

Her mother hurried to search for something for them to wear, and there was not a chance of talking about anything else.

All they best day-clothes and her mother's furs had been sold.

They were therefore unable to look as smart as they had last night.

When they went downstairs they were neat and tidy, if a little dowdy.

Mr. Dessoff seemed not to notice how they were dressed, he was smiling at her mother and paying her compliments.

By the time they reached the Restaurant where he was to give them luncheon Lady Milbanke was laughing.

Only when they had talked about anything except what Carla wanted to hear, they drove back to Islington.

As they turned into the Square where their house was situated, Carla saw with surprise that there was a carriage outside the house.

"Look, Mama!" she said. "Someone must be calling on us! I wonder who it is?"

"I think you will find," Mr. Dessoff replied before her mother could do so, "that it is the Dressmakers who I have ordered to bring you everything you require for the journey."

"What journey?" Carla questioned.

"I see your mother has not told you," Gustav Dessoff answered, "that I am taking you both to Vienna. We will be leaving early the day after tomorrow, and you and your mother must both be beautifully dressed, as she was when I first knew her."

Lady Milbanke made a little murmur, but she did not interrupt, and Mr. Dessoff went on:

"A Furrier will be arriving to see you later this afternoon. I have told him what furs you are to wear to accentuate your beauty."

Now Lady Milbanke said in a worried tone:

"Please . . you are making . . me embarrassed . . and Carla does not understand."

"I am sure she is as intelligent as she is lovely," Mr. Dessoff said, "and she will realise that what you are going to do is the only reasonable solution to your problems."

The carriage stopped and as they got out Mr. Dessoff said:

"Tonight I have an engagement which I cannot cancel, but tomorrow I will call for you at luncheon time, and expect to hear that everything I have arranged has gone according to plan."

"You are . . quite certain . . .?" Lady Milbanke began.

"Quite, quite certain," he interrupted. "Just leave everything to me."

He got back into the carriage and Carla followed her mother into the house.

The hall was filled with dress-boxes which they found were gradually being carried upstairs to Lady Milbanke's bedroom.

There were two Dressmakers waiting for them.

Both of whom, Carla knew, had shops in Bond Street which were patronised by all the most important hostesses in Mayfair.

They had each brought two assistants with them.

Before she even had time to speak to her mother Carla

found herself being fitted with day and evening-gowns, the bonnets, gloves and shoes which matched them.

The Furrier who arrived later brought them each a fur coat which made Carla gasp.

There were sables to replace those her mother had sold and an ermine cape to wear in the evening.

By the time the Dressmakers had left both Lady Milbanke and Carla were almost too tired to eat the delicious dinner which Bessie had prepared for them.

A glass of champagne, however, proved very reviving.

Only when they left the Dining-Room did Carla say:

"Please, Mama, you must explain what is happening."

They went into the Drawing-Room and Lady Milbanke clasping her hands together said:

"I am so . . afraid, darling . . that I am . . doing the . . wrong thing."

"What are you doing, Mama?"

"I thought . . you would have . . guessed," Lady Milbanke said in a low voice, "that I am going to . . sing at . . the Royal Opera House in Vienna!"

Carla stared at her.

"I thought what was happening must have something to do with your voice, but do you mean, Mama, that you are becoming a Prima Donna?"

"I suppose," Lady Milbanke said hesitatingly, "that is . . what I will be . . but I keep thinking how . . angry your father would be . . and how much he would . . disapprove of my . . singing in . . public."

"But, Mama, are you really good enough?" Carla asked.

"Gustav Dessoff thinks I am," her mother replied, "and he is the greatest entrepreneur in the . . whole world!"

Carla clasped her hands together.

"But, Mama, how wonderful! You will be famous and everybody will admire you, as I do."

Lady Milbanke rose from the chair in which she had been sitting.

She walked across the room and back again before she said:

"When your father heard me sing at a small private party given for His Majesty the King of Italy he . . swore that I . . should never sing . . again for . . anybody but . . him."

There was a pain in her voice.

Also the way she spoke which told Carla she was being torn in two by what she thought was wrong and the necessity of earning money.

"I am sure, if Papa knew how poor we were, and how hungry because we do not have enough to eat, he would understand," Carla said.

"Do you really think so?" Lady Milbanke asked. "He was always so . . insistent that my . . voice belonged to . . him and that . . no other man should . . hear it."

She gave a little sob, and Carla jumped up to put her arms around her mother.

"Now listen, Mama," she said, "I think what is happening is the answer to our prayers. I have prayed every night that somehow things would get better and we should not be so poor."

Her arms tightened round her mother and she gave a little laugh.

"I never thought for one moment that the answer would be this, but of course, it is the answer, and how could you possibly refuse it?"

"Is that what you . . really think?" her mother asked. "I too have prayed . . but we really have . . nothing left . . ."

Her voice broke, then through her tears she said:

"Now I can buy . . back my . . wedding ring."

"I am sure you will be able to afford a thousand rings now, Mama," Carla said. "It is wonderful, simply wonderful that Mr. Dessoff, like the genie in 'Aladdin' has come to our rescue."

"He is very kind," Lady Milbanke said, "and although I protested . . he has insisted on . . giving us all these . . wonderful clothes."

"Which we certainly need!" Carla exclaimed.

"I thought it was . . wrong to let him . . pay for . . them," her mother went on, "but he said that it was the same as . . dressing me for . . a part on the stage . . and he wanted . . everybody to be . . impressed by my . . appearance."

"He is quite right about that," Carla said, "and you certainly would not look very impressive in the rags you have been wearing lately."

"I realised this . . afternoon when we were . . trying on those lovely . . gowns how . . frightful we must have . . looked," Lady Milbanke said, "but now . . "

"Now," Carla interrupted, "everybody will know you are a star from the moment they see you, and that is exactly what you are, Mama, and as you sing like an angel, it is very appropriate!"

Lady Milbanke put her hand up to her throat.

"Mr. Dessoff says my voice is exactly the same, if not better than when he first heard it, and it is . . unique. He said it is a chance in a million to find a voice like mine."

"Then what would be the point of hiding it away," Carla asked, "and just singing to Bessie, me and the mice?"

Lady Milbanke gave a little laugh. Then she said:

"Oh . . Carla darling, I have to . . think about . . you in all this . . and that has . . worried me . . more than . . anything else."

"Of me? Why me?" Carla asked.

Her mother sat down on the sofa and drew her down beside her.

"This is going to be rather . . difficult where you are . . concerned."

"Why, Mama?"

"Because, darling, as your father's daughter, no one must know who you are, and more important, you must not fraternise with the actors and actresses or . . anybody in the . . Theatre."

Carla stared at her mother in astonishment.

"Why not?" she asked.

"Because, darling, your father would be horrified at you coming in contact with such people."

Lady Milbanke paused for a moment. Then she said:

"I have been thinking as to whom I could send you while I am in Vienna, but I can think of no one."

Carla gave a cry of horror.

"How can you suggest anything so cruel, so unkind?" she asked. "Of course I could not leave you! I am coming to Vienna! How could I stay behind?"

"I want you with me," Lady Milbanke said, "I want us to be together, but you must promise me, my darling . . on everything you hold . . sacred that you will do . . exactly as I tell you . . and keep . . out of . . sight."

She paused, and as Carla did not speak she went on:

"It means, I am afraid, that you will have a very dull life, except I know that Mr. Dessoff will be kind to you. But at least you will see Vienna which is a lovely City."

She put her hand on her daughter's arm as she said:

"When I am not at the Theatre, we can visit the Museums, the Cathedral and many other beautiful places which your father showed me when we were there years ago."

"I should love that, mama!" Carla said, "and do not

worry about me. I shall be quite happy, as long as I am with you."

"That is what I hoped you would say," Lady Milbanke replied, "but again I have to impress upon you that you are to have nothing to do with the stage, or the people on it."

"I shall have to see you perform, Mama!" Carla exclaimed.

"Of course you shall do that," her mother said, "but as part of the audience."

"I will applaud louder than anyone else!" Carla answered. "And think how exciting it will be!"

"It is exciting!" Lady Milbanke admitted. "At the same time, I am so . . afraid that it would . . prove wrong for . . you."

"I cannot think why it should be," Carla said.

"As soon as I have made enough money," Lady Milbanke said as if she was following her own train of thought, "we will come back to London, open the house and you can be presented at Buckingham Palace, as your father always planned."

There was a rapt note in her voice which Carla did not miss.

She knew her mother was really doing all this for her.

It was so that she could take her place in the Social World which he father had always enjoyed.

She thought that by the time her mother had made enough money to give up singing professionally and become a social hostess she would be getting much too old to be a débutante.

However, she did not say so, as she wanted her mother to be happy.

Alone in her bedroom, she told herself it was the most fortunate thing that could possibly happen.

"Thank You . . God . . thank You!" she said in the darkness. "We could not have gone on as we were, and this will be very exciting, and at least different from having nothing to do except wonder where our next meal would come from."

She said another prayer of gratitude.

Then because after so much excitement she was in fact, very tired, she fell asleep.

. . . .

The next morning there were more Dressmakers, more fittings, and it was a relief to be taken by Mr. Dessoff out to luncheon.

"I understand you have heard what I have planned for your mother," he said to Carla when he had ordered a delicious meal.

"She told me last night," Carla answered, "and I expect you realise you have arrived at exactly the right moment to save us from being so hungry that we would have had to eat what was left of the furniture!"

Lady Milbanke gave a little cry of protest, and Mr. Dessoff laughed.

"I cannot believe you would not have found a solution for yourselves," he said, "although perhaps not such a sensible one as mine."

His voice deepened as he said:

"I have often thought over the years what a wicked waste it was that your mother's voice was never allowed to be heard by those who would recognise it as unique."

"Is it really as good as that?" Carla asked curiously.

"I can swear on my honour," Mr. Dessoff replied, "that I have never in my long life heard a voice like it!"

He looked at Lady Milbanke and said:

"How could you do anything so selfish as to keep it all to yourself?"

"I kept if for my husband," she answered, "and of course, my daughter."

"I can only describe what you did as putting a cloud over the sun and never allowing it to shine on the world."

Carla laughed.

"Now you see, Mama, how important you are, and you always taught me that we each have something special to give to other people."

She looked at Mr. Dessoff to see if he understood, and explained:

"Mama did not mean money, but something of ourselves."

"And your mother must give her voice," he answered.

He threw out his hands in an expressive gesture as he said to Lady Milbanke:

"It was Fate that brought me to England at this particular moment, and I have found joy again. Now I feel like the man who sought the Golden Fleece!"

"Supposing I sing," Lady Milbanke said hesitatingly, "and no one is . . impressed and you have been . . mistaken?"

"I am prepared to stake my whole reputation that I am right," Gustav Dessoff replied, "and there are few men who will argue with me when I state that, in my opinion, your voice is the purest and most beautiful sound the world has ever heard!"

Carla clapped her hands.

"There, Mama! Now you cannot go on pretending to be modest about it, and you must be very careful that you do not catch cold."

"I will try not to," Lady Milbanke said as she put her hand on Mr. Dessoff's.

"I have not yet thanked you," she said, "for the fur coat you have given me, but it is far too generous, and I should not . . accept it."

"If without it you catch cold," he said, "that would be a disaster none of us dare contemplate."

Carla laughed at the mock horror in his voice and Lady Milbanke said:

"You are so kind, I do not know what to say."

"I do not need thanks from you," Mr. Dessoff replied. "I shall receive them from the critics and the audience."

"I hope you are right," Lady Milbanke said in a low voice.

Only when they returned home and were alone did Carla hug her mother and say:

"How can we be so lucky that you have this marvellous voice, and now everything is going to be different!"

She kissed her and went on:

"Stop worrying, Mama, and enjoy yourself. This is an adventure and suddenly I feel as if unexpectedly I have reached the top of the Himalyays, or discovered the North Pole!"

Lady Milbanke laughed.

"Oh, darling, it will be fun having you with me, and I will try not to be nervous."

"What have you to be nervous about?" Carla asked. "As you sing better than anybody else, why should you worry what they say, or what they think?"

She vowed later, as they set off, that she would do everything she could to prevent her mother from worrying.

Also to reassure here a dozen times a day that she was doing the right thing.

Her father had been so adamant that his wife should sing only for him.

Carla could therefore understand that it had been ingrained in her mother's mind that it was wrong to sing for others.

Lady Milbanke would feel this especially now that people would be paying to hear her.

Carla realised thiswas the difference between a professional and an amateur.

She thought a little cynically that, as her mother's voice was so unusual, it was a waste for it to be heard only by a few people.

There was so much to do before they left that Carla hardly had time to think about the future until they were on the train and speeding towards Vienna.

Mr. Dessoff had given her mother enough money to pay Bessie not only what she was owed.

She also received her wages for the next six months when she would take care of the house.

He had also instructed her, Carla discovered, that she was to buy back wherever possible, everything that had been sold.

He had arranged with a firm of Solicitors in London to pay any bill that Bessie presented to them.

He told Carla this, but he did not tell her mother.

"It is extremely kind of you," Carla said, "and I know Mama will be very, very grateful. At the same time, she will also be a little embarrassed that you should spend so much money on her."

"I would spend my entire fortune to have her sing for me," Mr. Dessoff said.

Then he added:

"If it worries her, she can pay me back when she receives the very large salary I am negotiating for her in Vienna, and it is what I shall do in every Opera House in which she performs."

Carla looked at him wide-eyed.

"Then you are not thinking of just staying in Vienna?"

"No, of course not," he replied, "your mother must be heard in Paris, Rome and eventually, perhaps even in – England."

He said the last word doubtfully and was obviously not surprised when Carla made a sound of protest.

"She will never sing in England where everybody knows her as Lady Milbanke," she said.

"That is in fact, what I thought myself," Mr. Dessoff replied, "but I said it to see your reaction to the suggestion."

"*I* would not mind," Carla said, "but it would upset Mama, and I am sure my father's relations would be very shocked.

"Tell me about his relations," Gustav Dessoff asked. "They do not seem to have done very much for your mother."

"That is true," Carla admitted, "but I think they were upset at my father marrying anyone so young, and also who was not entirely English."

Mr. Dessoff laughed.

"That is a very narrow-minded attitude, but true of a great number of your countrymen who feel completely separated from foreign contamination by the Channel!"

Carla thought this was very funny, and in a way it was true.

She understood why her mother was so insistent that no one must be aware of who she really was.

"I, of course, will be known by my maiden name of Ravello," she said, "and as both my father and mother are dead I do not think anyone in Italy will remember little Maria, who married when she was only seventeen."

"Am I to be Carla Ravello?" Carla enquired.

Her mother shook her head.

"I think it would be a mistake for me to admit to having my daughter with me. Journalists will want to interview me, and other people may wish to meet you."

"Then – who am I to be?" Carla enquired.

"I think you should just be a friend – a companion if you like, who travels with me."

"And my name?" Carla enquired.

"I have been thinking about that," her mother said, "and I am sure your father would be deeply hurt if you used any name but his. Banke is quite an ordinary English name, and 'Carla Banke' will not create any problems in a foreign capital."

"No, of course not, Mama, and it is always better to be truthful, if we can."

Lady Milbanke hesitated for a moment. Then she said:

"I am afraid, dearest, it will be very dull for you, but as I have said, as soon as I have made enough money, we will return to England, and you shall conquer the Social World in London, as I intend to conquer the Musical World, starting with Vienna!"

"I know who will receive the most applause," Carla said.

She was teasing her mother, but Lady Milbanke said seriously:

"What I want is for you to be admired and acclaimed as your father's daughter, and to find a man as handsome and attractive as he was who will love you as he loved me."

The way she spoke was very moving, and Carla said:

"That is what I want too, Mama, but we must not be greedy and ask for too many things at once. If you are a success, that is all that matters at the moment."

There was a little pause, then Lady Milbanke asked as she had asked a hundred times already:

"You, are sure, darling, I am doing the right thing!"

"Quite, quite sure," Carla replied, and her voice was very positive.

CHAPTER THREE

The journey to Vienna was comfortable; in fact Carla found that the hours passed by quickly, far quicker than she expected.

Mr. Dessoff had brought with him a large hamper of food and a crate of champagne.

This meant that they did not have to rely on the Restaurants at the Railway Stations.

Because Lady Milbanke had been worried, she was very tired.

Carla therefore encouraged her to sleep as much as possible.

She tucked her up in the pleasant compartment which was next to her one.

In their luggage which had been packed for them by the experienced assistants to the Dressmakers, there were two lace-trimmed cushions.

There were also a satin Alpaca rug with which she could cover her legs when she lay down during the day.

To Carla it was a delight to look at the beautiful gowns which Mr. Dessoff had given them and to know there were a great many more packed away in the Guard's van.

"How can we have been so fortunate that this has happened just when we were desperate?" she asked.

She said many prayers of thankfulness as she looked out of the window.

They passed through several different countries before they came to Austria.

They arrived in Vienna late in the afternoon.

As she might have expected, there were two carriages waiting for them at the station.

A Courier had accompanied them on their journey.

He apparently always looked after Mr. Dessoff and arranged everything on their arrival.

Lady Milbanke, Carla and Mr. Dessoff got into the first carriage and drove away immediately.

"I am taking you to stay at a new Hotel which was opened only last year," Mr. Dessoff explained, "and I think you will find it delightful."

Carla realised that her mother was hardly listening but looking out of the window.

She was sure she was thinking of the last time she had been in Vienna with her father.

Because she felt it was a little inconsiderate to Mr. Dessoff, when he had been so kind, she gave him all her attention.

"A new Hotel!" she exclaimed. "I thought everything in Vienna was very old."

"Most of it is," Mr. Dessoff agreed with a smile, "but the Sacher Hotel was built after the opening of the new Opera House in 1868."

'So there is a new Opera House since my mother was here,' Carla thought, but she did not interrupt as Mr. Dessoff went on:

"Despite the protests of the whole Viennese population, the old Kärntnertor Theatre was demolished, and a modern Hotel built in its place."

"And that is where we are going to now?" Carla asked.

"Yes, you are," Mr. Dessoff said. "And it is kept by a brilliant young man who invented the famous 'Sacher Torte' or cake. Surely you remember that, my dear?"

With a start Lady Milbanke realised he was speaking

to her and she turned from looking out of the window to reply:

"Yes, of course! It is delicious! I remember feeling very greedy when I was here because I ate so much of it!"

"Why is it so extraordinary?" Carla asked.

"It was invented by a boy of sixteen called Franz Sacher, for the Prince Metternich," Mr. Dessoff answered.

Carla had of course heard of the greatest Statesman Austria had ever had, and Mr. Dessoff went on:

"It seems incredible, but young Sacher put something secret into the cake which makes it so exceptional. But no one knows what it is."

"You are making me feel hungry," Carla laughed.

"You shall have some as soon as we arrive," Mr. Dessoff promised.

The Sacher Hôtel was very impressive, and they were shown into what Carla was sure was the most important Suite in the whole building.

It was on a corner with a delightful Sitting-Room.

The carved white chairs, sofa and table were an attractive contrast to the rose-pink curtains and carpet.

There were masses of flowers which Carla guessed Mr. Dessoff had ordered for her mother.

There was also open on the table a white box containing a Sacher cake.

"Now, eat and enjoy yourself!" Mr. Dessoff said.

Carla thought no one could be more kind and considerate.

Because she was tired after the journey, Lady Milbanke said she would lie down.

Mr. Dessoff explained as the luggage was brought up that he had already engaged a lady's-maid who would look after her.

Named Anna she would also accompany Carla if she wanted to explore the City and look at the shops.

"You have thought of everything!" Lady Milbanke said putting out her hand.

"I think of you," Mr. Dessoff replied, "and most of all, your voice!"

He raised her hand to his lips and told them he would return at eight o'clock to give them dinner in a private room.

The lady's-maid was middle-aged and very competent.

She spoke French as well as German and even a little English.

"I have maided many important ladies who have visited Vienna, *Madame*," she said to Lady Milbanke, "and I hope I will give you every satisfaction."

"I am sure you will," Lady Milbanke replied, "and it is a great delight not to have to do anything for myself."

"No, no, *Madame*," the maid replied. "Herr Dessoff has explained that you must take things easy, and rest as much as possible."

Carla left her mother in Anna's capable hands and as Lady Milbanke undressed and got into bed, she went to her own room.

It was on the other side of the Sitting-Room, and while smaller than her mother's, was still beautifully furnished with pictures in gold frames on the walls.

There was also a small chandelier hanging from the painted ceiling.

"It is all so romantic," she said to herself.

Then she remembered there would be no romance for her in Vienna as she had to be very discreet and keep out of sight.

She thought, however, that she would tell herself stories when she visited the Museums and the famous Stephansdom Cathedral.

Perhaps too she would be able to peep at the Prater.

Her mother had told her that is where the Viennese disported themselves with every sort of amusement like there was in England when there was a Circus.

Mr. Dessoff arrived at eight o'clock, looking very smart in his evening clothes.

Lady Milbanke and Carla were ready and waiting for him.

They were wearing one of the new gowns he had given them, and which seemed too smart for just an evening alone with an elderly man.

They went down the stairs to the private room where they were to dine.

As they passed through the Reception Hall, a man who was walking from the house at the far end of it stopped.

"Good-evening, *Herr* Dessoff," he said. "I thought I should see you in Vienna."

For a moment, Mr. Dessoff looked at him uncertainly. Then he said:

"It is Baron Otto von Erhardt, I think?"

"Correct," the Gentleman replied, "and if you remember, we met two years ago in Berlin."

"Yes, yes, of course," Mrs. Dessoff said.

While the two men were talking, Lady Milbanke had moved a little further down the passage.

It was where they were going before the Baron had intercepted them.

Carla was just about to follow her when the Baron said:

"It is delightful to see you, and I hope you will introduce me to yòur friends."

"They have only just arrived and are very tired," Mr. Dessoff replied evasively, "so forgive me if I say good-night, *Herr* Baron, and I hope we meet another time."

He turned away, took hold of Carla by the arm and drew her quickly down the passage after her mother.

The private room was at the end of it and there was a *Mâitre d'Hôtel* waiting to welcome them.

A waiter was already pouring out the champagne.

"I think it would be a mistake," Lady Milbanke said in a low tone, "to meet your friend, until we are settled in."

"He is no friend of mine!" Mr. Dessoff said, "in fact, I dislike the man."

"Then we must hope we do not see him again," Lady Milbanke said, and started to talk of other things.

The meal was excellent, in fact even better than those they had enjoyed in the Restaurants in London.

Carla could hear music coming very softly in the distance.

She thought it must be playing in the Restaurant, and that it was a pity they could not have dined there.

She had thought the Baron was good-looking in a heavy, Germanic way.

But she could understand that Mr. Dessoff was anxious to keep her mother to himself.

At least until she had accepted the fact that she was no longer Lady Milbanke, but Maria Ravello.

As if he realised what she was thinking he said:

"Tomorrow I will take your mother to the Opera House, and you must enjoy yourself exploring the City. Anna will go with you, and you do understand, my dear, that you must never go out alone.'

"Yes, of course," Carla replied. "Bessie always accompanied me when we were in London, if Mama was too tired to do so."

Mr. Dessoff looked at her a long moment, then sighed:

"As your mother cannot be here with you," he said,

"you will have to be very circumspect in looking after yourself."

Carla looked surprised, and he went on:

"The Viennese are very easily infatuated with a beautiful face, and I expect men will try to talk to you, but you must just walk away, and not take any notice of what they say."

"I understand," Carla replied. "But will you arrange that I can watch Mama in the Theatre?"

"Yes, of course," Mr. Dessoff said. "There will be no hurry as first she has to meet Franz Jauner."

"Who is he?" Carla asked.

"Franz Jauner is the Director of the Royal Opera House," he answered. "He is a Viennese who was appointed last year, and I am predicting that he will be the most brilliant Director the Vienna Opera has ever had."

"He sounds interesting," Carla said.

"He is to the Music World," Mr. Dessoff agreed, "and I know when I tell him I have brought your mother to Vienna, he will go down on his knees in gratitude."

"Tell me more about him," Carla begged.

"At the moment he is doing something very imaginative and very unusual," Mr. Desoff replied. "Last year he not only brought Wagner's exquisite work to the stage, but also arranged that Wagner himself should conduct it."

"That must have been an excitement!" Carla exclaimed.

"It was!" Mr. Dessoff agreed, "and now Jauner is preparing to produce '*Die Walküre* and your mother must take part in it."

"Then I must certainly see the 'Ride of the Valkyries'."

"You shall!" Mr. Dessoff smiled. "Jauner has engaged the Empress Elisabeth's riding teacher to help in the production, and I feel sure it will be extremely dramatic."

"Please, do not forget me," Carla pleaded.

He smiled as he replied:

"That would be impossible, although I think there may be problems in having two such beautiful ladies under my care at the same time."

Carla thought he was only paying her a compliment and did not take him seriously.

When they had finished dinner Mr. Dessoff advised her mother to retire to bed.

She agreed and they walked back along the passage to the stairs which led to their Suite.

When they reached the Reception Hall, as if by chance, Baron Otto von Erhardt was coming from the Lounge.

With him was a very attractive woman who was exquisitely dressed and wearing a great deal of jewellery.

He immediately walked up to Mr. Dessoff and said:

"I have been wondering, Dessoff, whether you would be able to dine with me tomorrow night, and of course bring your friends with you."

"Thank you, *Herr Baron*, it is very kind of you," Mr. Dessoff replied, "but I regret that is impossible."

He bowed and hurried Lady Milbanke towards the stairs.

Carla was behind them, and the Baron was able to speak to her.

"As Mr. Dessoff omitted to introduce us," he said, "may I present myself?"

Remembering what she had been told, Carla dropped him a small curtsy and said:

"I am sorry, but I must go up to my . . ."

She was just about to say "My mother" when she remembered and stammered instead: ". . . friend."

Then she was running up the stairs.

She caught up with her mother and Mr. Dessoff before they reached the first landing.

Anna was waiting for them and Mr. Dessoff said goodnight.

There was no chance of Carla talking to her mother until she was undressed.

Then when she was wearing a nightgown and a very pretty negligèe she went into her mother's room.

There were two candles alight by the bed and Lady Milbanke was nearly asleep.

"Goodnight, my dearest," she said, "it is all very exciting but I am very tired."

"Of course you are, Mama."

Carla kissed her and for a moment her mother held her close.

"I do hope . . your father is not . . angry with me for . . coming here," she said almost in a whisper.

"All you have to think about, Mama, is being a success," Carla said. "How could you disappoint Mr. Dessoff, after he has given us such beautiful clothes and we have had such a comfortable journey here?"

"He is very, very kind," Lady Milbanke agreed.

Then as she shut her eyes Carla blew out the candles and went to her own room.

She was not really sleepy so she pulled back the curtains, raised the blind and looked out of the window at the lighted streets.

There were quite a number of smart carriages driving past.

She thought how exciting it would be if she was going somewhere where she could dance, perhaps to the wonderful Waltzes that had been composed by Johann Strauss.

Then she told herself she was being selfish.

All she should be thinking about was her mother and

how to help her make the money which would enable them to return to London.

At the same time, she felt she could hear music being played softly in the distance.

She wondered if the Baron was dancing somewhere with the attractive lady who had been with him.

"Tomorrow I will buy a book and read all about Vienna," Carla decided, "and perhaps it will be possible, although I am not certain how, to watch some of the dancing, even if I cannot dance myself."

Resolutely she pulled down the blind, shut the curtains and got into bed.

The next morning they had breakfast late in their Suite.

They had only just finished when Mr. Dessoff was announced.

Even before he spoke Carla knew that everything was going smoothly and he had brought good news.

Having kissed Lady Milbanke's hand he sat down beside her and said:

"Franz Jauner is ecstatic at the idea of you appearing in *Die Walküre*. I have asked him only for a small part to start with, so that you would not feel nervous, but could become accustomed to singing in an Opera House."

"I shall be . . very nervous," Lady Milbanke said.

"Once you begin to sing you will forget your nerves, and there will be no problem."

He smiled at her reassuringly and said:

"I am going to take you now to meet *Herr* Jauner and to see the magnificent Opera House which is without its peer in the whole of Europe."

Lady Milbanke looked frightened.

"What shall I . . wear?" she asked a little helplessly.

"You will look lovely in whatever you put on," Mr.

Dessoff replied. "But I am sure your daughter understands that first impressions are always important."

Carla rose to her feet.

"Come along, Mama," she said, "you have to make a grand entrance and when you try, no one can do that better than you."

She dressed her mother in one of the very beautiful gowns which Mr. Dessoff had given them in England.

Then she wrapped the ermine stole round her shoulders, and thought that no one could look more lovely, and more spectacular.

The bonnet which matched Lady Milbanke's gown was trimmed with tiny curled ostrich feathers which framed her face.

Mr. Dessoff obviously thought that his protégée was exactly as he wished.

Before he took Lady Milbanke downstairs to where the carriage was waiting, he said to Carla:

"We will be back for luncheon, but if by any chance our plans are changed, I will send you a message."

"Thank you," Carla said. "Good luck!"

She kissed her mother saying:

"Do not worry about anything, Mama! You look absolutely beautiful and when they hear you sing they will think of nothing else."

When she was alone, Carla went into the bedroom to find Anna.

"I would like to go for a walk, Anna," she said.

"Yes, of course, *Fräulein*," Anna agreed. "I'll be finished in *Madame's* bedroom in about ten minutes."

It was actually a little longer before they went downstairs.

Carla was wearing the fur coat which Mr. Dessoff had given her to travel in.

Although the sun was shining there was frost on the air.

The walked to the shops which were not far from the Hotel.

Carla also learned that the Royal Opera house was only a very short distance away.

"It is certainly very convenient, that we are right at the heart of things," she said to Anna.

"That's what I was thinking, *Fräulein*," Anna agreed.

They looked at a number of shops, then Carla insisted on going to the cathedral.

She thought she would light a candle and say a prayer of thankfulness that they had come to Vienna.

She also wanted to pray that her mother would be the success Mr. Dessoff expected.

St. Stephen's Cathedral, or what the Viennese called the Stephansdom, was very old, but very impressive.

Carla thought she could feel the vibrations of faith from the generations of Viennese who had worshipped in the ancient building for centuries.

There were many people lighting the candles in front of the Statues of the Saints.

The beauty of the stained glass windows and music being played softly on the organ made Carla feel that she was very close to God.

Her mother, being half-Italian, was a Catholic, but her father had been a Protestant.

They had made a pact when they were married that if they had a son he would be baptised in the Church of England, but a daughter would follow her mother's religion.

Carla had therefore been baptised a Catholic.

Because she loved her father she had often attended Services with him.

There were the Churches which were always to be found near the Embassies to which he was attached in various countries.

As far as she was concerned there was only one God,

and whenever she prayed He listened to her and had answered all her prayers.

When she left the Stephansdom there was a radiance in her face that came from her soul.

Although she was not aware of it, she looked so beautiful that many people stopped to look at her.

There was one man in particular who was just going into the Cathedral as she emerged.

Carla did not see him, but when she stopped to look up at the sky as she came through the West Door he too stood still.

He watched her as if spellbound.

Then Anna realised that time was passing and Lady Milbanke would be back for luncheon.

She hurried Carla back to the Hôtel the way they had come.

. . . .

"Everybody was so charming to me!" Lady Milbanke said when Carla joined her, "and this afternoon I am going to a rehearsal, not to perform – I will do that tomorrow – but to watch the 'Ride of the Valkyries' with which apparently they are having a little trouble."

"Oh, Mama, let me come too!" Carla begged.

Lady Milbanke looked at Mr. Dessoff.

"You shall both sit in a box," he said. "Then if later, Maria, you come down onto the stage, Carla will be safe until we return."

Carla clapped her hands with excitement and could hardly manage to eat any luncheon because she was so thrilled.

As the Royal Opera House was so near Lady Milbanke suggested that instead of using Mr. Dessoff's carriage, they might walk there.

"I really need some exercise, and some fresh air," she said, "and it is such a short way."

"Very well," Mr. Dessoff agreed, "but wrap up warmly for, although the sun is shining at the moment, it will turn colder as the day draws on."

Lady Milbanke and Carla put on their fur coats and set off to walk with Mr. Dessoff to the Royal Opera House.

They had nearly reached it when just ahead of them a man driving a very smart Chaise was having some trouble with one of his horses.

They could not cross the road until he had passed them, so stayed on the pavement watching him.

He was a handsome, very smartly dressed young man.

Carla realised from the way he handled his reins that he was an expert driver.

Finally he had the obstreperous horse under control and started to move on his way.

As he did so he realised that three people had been watching him.

He turned to smile at them as if apologising for the delay.

Then as his eyes met Carla's he swept off his hat.

She smiled at him because she could not help herself, then when he had driven on and they crossed the road Mr. Dessoff said dryly:

"You have obviously made a conquest, my dear!"

Carla laughed.

"He is an excellent driver, just as my father was."

Ahead of them was a side door of the Opera House to which Mr. Dessoff was taking them.

They went inside and the building was far larger and more impressive than Carla had expected.

They walked up a wide staircase which she felt had been specially built for the route to the Royal Box.

She was therefore not surprised to find the box into which they were shown was near to it.

Carla looked round her.

The gold and red of the ornate boxes and the huge chandeliers falling from a high ceiling were breathtaking.

The box into which Mr. Dessoff took them was in the Royal circle.

On the stage the curtains were drawn back.

While there were workmen and scene-shifters moving about, Carla could easily imagine how it could hold three-hundred people.

As for the Valkyries and their horses there would be no problem.

She had learned at Luncheon that the Riding Master to the Empress had managed to commandeer eight Army horses.

He also had invited eight Polish horsemen to act as the Valkyries' doubles.

Carla was wondering how they would 'ride through the air' but was certain that however it was done, it would be very dramatic.

As they sat down she realised that her mother was thinking not of the Valkyries but of the Theatre and her own part in it.

"It is . . so large!" Lady Milbanke said nervously.

"Your voice will fill it," Mr. Dessoff said quietly, "and when you sing there will be silence from those who will enjoy every note!"

He was saying all the right things, Carla thought, to make her mother happy.

The workmen began to leave the stage and Mr. Dessoff said:

"I want you to come down, my dear, and see everything as an actress and not as a spectator."

"Of course," Lady Milbanke agreed. "I will do whatever . . you want."

She rose and leaving her coat on the chair in which she had been sitting, took Mr. Dessoff's arm as he led her out of the box.

When they had gone Carla realised it was warm in the Theatre and took off her own coat.

She then discovered there were pegs in the back of the box on which she could hang hers and her Mother's coats.

Having done so, she sat down in the best seat from which she could watch the stage.

She realised everything would look very different when the lights were on and the chandeliers lit.

She knew the boxes would be filled with ladies glittering with tiaras and men resplendent in evening clothes.

She hoped at the performance when her mother sang that the Emperor and Empress would be there to hear her.

Perhaps afterwards she might be introduced to them.

'If that happens,' she thought with a smile, 'Mama will find it difficult to remember that she is now Maria Ravello, and not Papa's wife!'

She knew how many Royalties her mother and father had met when he was at the various British Embassies.

She thought that at least her mother would know how to behave and not be nervous socially.

The rehearsal began, and she was thrilled not only by the music, but by what was happening on the stage.

It was no surprise to realise that Franz Jauner had worked out a very complicated but effective ride for the 'Valkyries'.

The Polish Army riders were dressed in wigs and helmets.

In the background an approach was cleared for the

horses between wisps of cloud and there were thick mattresses to deaden the sound of their hoofs.

Later Carla was to learn that the horses started the 'Ride' from the stage-door on the *Kärntnerstrasse* side and 'landed' on the opposite one on the *Opemgasse* side.

At this moment she only realised that across the Valkyries's saddles were strung outside dummies.

They represented Wagner's 'Fallen heroes' on their way to Valhalla.

She also saw that *Grane* who was Brünnhilde's steed, was giving a lot of trouble by refusing to stand still while they were rehearsing.

This was in Act II when she was telling Seigmund he is to go to Valhalla with her.

The rehearsal was stopped while Jauner coped with this problem.

He stationed a soldier from the Army Service Corps behind a rock and provided the horse with a liberal supply of oats.

Carla was so intent on what she was watching, thinking it fantastic, that she did not hear the door of the Opera Box open behind her.

Then she started when a deep voice said:

"I see, *Fräulein*, that you are as interested in the stage horses as you were in mine."

Carla looked round and saw the young man she had watched controlling his horse outside the Opera House.

He was standing inside the box holding his tall hat in his hand.

She thought he was even more handsome than she had thought when she first saw him.

Because she was so surprised at his sudden appearance she forgot she had been told to speak to no one, and answered him by saying:

"I thought you handled your horse exceptionally well, considering how difficult he was being!"

"That is the sort of compliment I like to receive," the young man said, "and horses can always be a problem, as Brünnhilde's steed is being at the moment."

"I can see that Mr. Jauner is arranging for him to have oats behind a rock," Carla smiled, "and I think it is a very clever idea."

"So do I," the Young Man agreed. "May I sit down and watch what happens next?"

He sat down next to her as he spoke.

It was only then that Carla realised if she had obeyed her mother's instructions she should have told him to go away.

Because it seemed rude to do so, she merely smiled and asked:

"Why are you at the rehearsal?"

"If you are accusing me of sneaking in," he replied. "I can explain my presence quite simply: one of my horses is taking part in the Show."

Carla looked at the stage, then back again at the Young Man who was speaking.

"Please, do tell me which one!" she begged.

"The second from the left," he replied. "He is waiting for instructions."

"I can see from here that he is very fine, like the horses you were driving."

"The one on the stage is the charger I have ridden for five years," the young man explained.

"So you are in the Army!" Carla said.

"Not now, but I was at one time, and as I possess a number of very well trained horses, the riding Instructor who is teaching the Valkyries what to do, asked if I would be kind enough to let him have my most experienced horse to guide the others."

"Looking at him I am sure that he will do beautifully!" Carla cried.

"And now, tell me why you are here," the young man asked.

Carla was silent for a moment, then she said:

"It is . . very embarrassing for me to say so . . but I was told by Mr. Dessoff and by m.my . . my friend . . not to speak to . . anyone."

The young man smiled.

"That is exactly the instruction I should have given you myself in their place! But now I am here, and we have been talking and you cannot 'put back the clock'."

"That is . . true," Carla admitted.

"Then as there is no one to notice us," he said, "suppose you tell me your name."

"It is . . Carla."

She gave him only her Christian name because for the moment she was thinking whether or not she should explain who her mother was.

Then she decided it would be best for him to remain in ignorance.

"Mine is Rákóczi," he replied, "but my friends always call me 'Rákó'."

"Rákóczi!" Carla exclaimed, "I know that name!"

She thought for a moment, then she said:

"I think, unless I am mistaken, that Prince Rákóczi in the 17th century was one of the great romantic heroes of Hungarian history!"

Rákó clapped his hands.

"You are quite right! He was, and I am very proud to bear his name."

"Then you are Hungarian!" Carla said, "and of course Hungarian horses are famous, which is why yours is so outstanding!"

"I give you full marks!" Rákó said, "but I am surprised to find an English girl should know so much about Hungarian history!"

"And I am surprised that a Hungarian should speak such good English!" Carla said quickly.

"Shall I say I was as well-educated as you have obviously been," Rákó answered.

"I long to go to Hungary," Carla said dreamily. "I have heard how beautiful it is."

"Beautiful, wild, and wonderful for horses," Rákó replied, "and being English, of course you ride well."

"I like to think so," Carla smiled, "but not as well as the Empress Elisabeth who everybody knows, is happier in Hungary than anywhere else."

"That is true," Rákó replied, "and I have never seen anyone ride as well as Her Majesty!"

Carla drew in her breath.

"Are you saying you have . . seen her?"

There was silence for a moment. Then Rákò said:

"Perhaps one morning I could smuggle you into the Riding School when she is practising with the Spanish horses which of course you will have heard about."

"Of course I have!" Carla said. "Oh, if you could do that, it would be the most . . wonderful thing that could ever . . happen to me!"

Even as she spoke she felt sure it was something of which her mother would not approve of her doing.

Therefore, even if she received the invitation she would have to refuse it.

She looked away from Rákó and to her surprise he must have read her thoughts, for he said:

"Sometimes one has to be adventurous and forget the conventions!"

She looked at him wide-eyed.

"How did you know that was worrying me?"

"Your eyes are very expressive," he said, "and also from the moment I first saw you, I knew that I had to find you again, and that is what I have done!"

Carla did not reply and he went on:

"I saw you this morning coming out of the Stephansdom and I thought you had, for the moment, been carried away into the sky, and had not yet come back to earth!"

"How could you . . possibly have . . known that," Carla asked.

"I have never before seen anyone who looked as if they had been with the angels," Rákó replied.

Carla drew in her breath.

Then as her eyes met Rákó's she was suddenly afraid.

"Please," she said quickly, "go away! My . . friend will be returning soon, and it will be . . difficult to explain why we are . . talking here together."

She thought for a moment that he would refuse. Then he said:

"I will do what you ask me on one condition, that you tell me where you are staying so that I can find you again."

"We are at the Sacher Hôtel," Carla replied, "but . . please . . you must not . . come there . . or communicate with . . me."

She thought as she spoke that she was presuming that was what he wanted to do, and he said quite simply:

"Fate is on our side, and I promise we shall meet again."

He rose to his feet before he added:

"If only when I take you to see the Empress riding."

Carla drew in her breath. Then she said:

"You are . . tempting me to behave . . badly when I am trying to be . . good, and do as I am . . told."

He looked down at her for a moment.

"Because I think you are good," he said, "I promise I will not do anything that you would think was wrong or bad. But can anyone resist horses and horsemanship?"

Because it was something she had not expected him to say, Carla laughed.

Rákó walked to the door.

"I am leaving now because you have asked me to do so," he said, "but do not forget me until we meet again."

He did not wait for an answer but went out of the box closing the door behind him.

For a moment Carla wanted to call him back.

She felt she had so much more to say to him, and so much to hear.

Especially if he could tell her about Hungary and whether he could smuggle her into the Spanish Riding School.

Then she told herself she must behave with propriety and she had already broken the rules in talking to a man she did not know.

"The last thing I must do at the moment is to worry Mama," she told herself.

Then she knew she was only making excuses for her own behaviour.

When she thought about it, how could she do anything else?

She knew that meeting Rákó had been very exciting, and something she had never expected could happen in Vienna.

CHAPTER FOUR

Soon after Rákó had left Lady Milbanke and Mr. Dessoff returned.

"It is a very, very large stage!" Lady Milbanke said to Carla. "I felt lost on it!"

"It will not seem so big when you are singing," Mr. Dessoff said comfortingly, "and anyway, when you rehearse tomorrow morning you can make any suggestion you want.'

Lady Milbanke gave him a grateful smile, then they returned to the Hôtel.

Carla realised that there was a lot her mother wanted to discuss with Mr. Dessoff.

She therefore went to her bedroom.

Alone, she thought of how easy it had been to talk with Rákó, and how interesting he was.

She did not really believe that he could take her to see the Empress ride.

If he did it would be the most exciting thing she could imagine.

She had always had a tremendous admiration for the Empress.

She had read everything she could find about her in the books and newspapers in the different countries she had visited with her father.

Some of them, especially in France, where they were indiscreet about Royal households, said the Empress was very happy.

She hated, they wrote, being in Vienna, and only enjoyed being in Hungary.

Carla wondered if this was true.

She could understand that the Empress, with her love of horses, would adore being able to ride the magnificent Hungarian stallions.

They were acclaimed everywhere as being the best in Europe.

It was fascinating to feel that now she was in Vienna she was near the Empress and might see her.

Perhaps she would see her driving out from the Schönbrunn Palace looking as beautiful as everybody said she was.

At the same time, she might also be sad and subdued.

She was undoubtedly living in what was known as a stiff and pompous Court.

She was also reported to be persecuted by her Mother-in-Law.

'I must see her,' Carla thought.

Then she told herself it would be very reprehensible to do what Rákó had suggested and would undoubtedly shock her mother.

"I must not worry Mama at the moment," she admonished herself, "when she is already nervous at having to sing in public."

Carla thought actually it was very brave of her mother to even contemplate singing on that enormous stage.

What was more it would be to an extremely critical audience.

The Viennese lived, breathed and thought music, and it was indivisibly part of their very existence.

"Whatever I do, I will do nothing which might distress Mama," Carla decided.

Later, she heard Mr. Dessoff leave and went into the Sitting-Room.

She found her mother reading the score of what she would sing tomorrow.

"Are you not going to practise it, Mama?" Carla asked.

Her mother shook her head.

"Mr. Dessoff said if I wished to do so he would have a piano brought here, but he thought that after the journey I ought to rest my voice because I am still tired."

"Of course, that is very sensible," Carla approved, "and if you are sure, Mama, you should undress and have dinner in bed."

"I will do that," Lady Milbanke agreed.

Carla rang for Anna and when she came she helped Lady Milbanke out of her clothes.

Carla had tea with her mother.

When it was time for dinner she peeped into her bedroom and saw that she was fast asleep.

'It would be a mistake to wake her,' she thought, 'and if the waiters bring my dinner into the Sitting-Room she will hear them moving about.'

She therefore told Anna to go downstairs and say that she would have a small dinner in the private room where they had dined last night.

She knew that Mr. Dessoff had arranged it should be at their disposal for as long as they were in the Hôtel.

When she had changed for dinner, wearing one of the pretty gowns they had brought from London, she thought it was rather sad that she would be alone.

She would have liked to have someone to talk to.

Because she was still intent on protecting her mother, she tip-toed into the Sitting-Room.

She peeped into her bedroom to be quite certain she was asleep.

Then she went downstairs.

When she entered the private room she saw there was a waiter there and the table was laid for two.

"I am afraid there has been some mistake," she said. "*Madame* Ravello is asleep and I am dining alone."

She spoke in French, thinking perhaps the men would understand it better than English.

As she did so someone came into the room and she saw with surprise, that it was the Baron.

"Good evening, Miss Banke!" he said. "I learned you were dining alone, and as I was doing the same I thought it would be very much more congenial and certainly more friendly, if we dined together!"

He was speaking in quite good English, even though he had a decided German accent.

As he finished speaking, the waiter offered Carla a glass of wine and another to the Baron.

Carla took the glass automatically. She was wondering how she could tell him she had no intention of dining with him.

"I have been told by the Concierge," he went on, "that your friend is Maria Ravello, and that Gustav Dessoff who is undeniably an authority, declares she has a voice that will astound Vienna!"

The Baron was so much at his ease and talking so confidently that Carla found it hard to put into words what she wanted to say.

He smiled at her before he continued:

"You cannot be so cruel and unkind as to refuse my company when we have so much to say to each other and I will be very hurt and also very angry if you send me away."

It flashed through Carla's mind that because he was over-powering and very sure of himself he would be a bad enemy.

He might therefore hurt her mother.

She was well aware that the one thing that would distress her more than anything else would be if anyone in Vienna should know who she really was.

Someone like the Baron, who had obviously made enquiries about them both, might inadvertently learn the truth.

Carla hesitated. She was afraid and did not know what to do.

The Baron however settled himself in one of the arm-chairs in front of the fire.

"Now," he said, "let us enjoy this delicious wine which I have ordered specially, and I hope you will appreciate the menu I have chosen."

He was taking a great deal upon himself, Carla thought, but she did not know what she could do about it.

Reluctantly she sat down in a chair opposite him.

As she did so she felt there was something impertinent about the way he looked at her.

It was almost as if he was appraising her.

His eyes seemed to take in the colour of her hair, her heart-shaped face and the curve of her breasts.

She had an almost instintive impulse to jump up and run from the room.

Then she thought it would be over-dramatic.

It would also be undoubtedly a story which the waiters would repeat to each other.

Perhaps the other guests in the Hôtel might get to hear of it.

What was more, it would leave the Baron looking foolish, and he would consider it an insult.

She had the feeling that, as he was a Prussian, he would want his revenge.

In a voice that sounded rather young and helpless she therefore said:

"You have taken me by surprise, *Herr Baron*, and I am not certain if it is correct for us to dine together."

"What is correct," he replied, "is for you to enjoy your dinner with me."

She did not answer and he went on:

"You are very lovely, and the moment I saw you, I knew that I had to get to know you better."

He laughed.

"Dessoff was being very possessive about you and also Maria Ravello, which does not surprise me, but I am not so easily defeated!"

'No, I am . . sure you are . . not!" Carla said.

She was thinking he was boasting in a somewhat aggressive manner.

The Baron drank down his wine and raised his glass so that the waiter at the other end of the room would know that he wished it to be re-filled.

"Now, tell me about yourself," he said in a caressing tone. "I have learned that you are a friend and a companion of Dessoff's mysterious songster, but you look very young for such a position."

It struck Carla that he thought she was being paid for what she did.

She raised her chin a little before she replied:

"*Madame* Ravello is someone I have known and loved and I feel I am very fortunate to accompany her to Vienna."

"It is very fortunate for me that you are here," the Baron said.

He bent forward as he spoke and Carla decided that she disliked him.

She had the feeling he was encroaching, if not menacing her, and she wished the evening was already over.

She put down her glass from which she had taken only a small sip and said:

"Surely our dinner is ready, and I am hungry!"

"Then we will eat," the Baron said.

He gave the order sharply to the waiter, then put out his hand to help Carla to her feet.

As he touched her she felt herself shiver.

She knew that she was right in thinking he was unpleasant.

She had been quite young, when she had first known that she could 'feel' the vibrations of people she met.

She knew even without talking to them, what they were like.

"That man who came here today is bad and dangerous!" she said once to her father. "You must be very careful of him, Papa!"

Lord Milbanke had stared at her in astonishment.

"What makes you say that?" he asked.

"I can feel it!" she had replied.

Her father had been silent for a moment before he said:

"You are absolutely right, and I would not have had him in the house if he had not asked himself. And yet, because he is of such Social importance, I am surprised that you realise what he is like beneath that highly polished veneer."

After that Carla had often talked to her father about his guests.

He had to admit, although she had sat quietly at luncheon and had not even spoken to them, she was usually right in summing up their characters.

Now dinner began and the Baron helped himself to a very large portion of every dish.

She knew as he did so he was a man she would find it difficult to avoid, even though she had every intention of trying.

It was unfortunate that he was staying at the same Hôtel.

It would therefore be more difficult not to see him than if he was elsewhere.

As the meal progressed the Baron talked about himself.

It was quite obvious to Carla he was trying to impress

her with his importance, his possessions and his position, both at the Court of Berlin and socially.

"There are many things I would like to show you in my country," he said, "but that is something we must talk about a little later."

Carla did not say that she had visited Berlin once with her father and mother.

She had thought the formality and the Germans themselves were very unlike the elegance and the witty intelligence of the French.

They also had none of the warmth and friendliness of the Italians.

It took a long time to eat the lengthy and elaborate meal at which the Baron had drunk an enormous amount.

However, the Baron ordered a brandy for himself and insisted, although she had refused, on her having a sweet liqueur with the coffee.

She had no intention of drinking it.

But as the Baron would not take 'No' for an answer, she allowed the wine waiter to set a small glass on the table in front of her.

Then the waiters left the room and the Baron said:

"Now, lovely little lady, tell me about yourself for, as you can imagine, I am very curious."

Carla did not reply: in fact she had said very little during the whole meal.

"How many men have been in love with you?" he questioned. "I assure you I am very jealous of my predecessors."

"I do not know what you are talking about," Carla said coldly, "and as it is getting late, I am sure *Madame* Ravello is awake and will want me to be with her."

"That is nonsense, as you well know," the Baron said. "If we go very quietly to your bedroom, I am sure she will not hear us!"

Carla stared at him for a moment not understanding what he had said.

Then as she saw an expression in his eyes, she drew in her breath.

"I think, *Herr Baron*," she said, "you are insulting me!"

She put down her coffee-cup as she spoke and would have risen to her feet, but the Baron laughed and said:

"If you think I would let you go you are very much mistaken! You have captivated me, you beautiful creature, and I am determined, absolutely determined, that you shall be mine!"

Carla rose, then as she turned towards the door the Baron, without rising to his feet put out his hand and caught her wrist.

"You are shy," he said. "I find that not only exciting, but it also makes me think that no other man has possessed you."

Carla tried to pull herself free of him.

But his fingers were like a clamp round her slim wrist.

Then he said:

"Do not be a little fool! I will give you everything you want: a house of your own, horses, jewels, and enough money to buy the moon, if you want it!"

Because what he said horrified her, Carla managed to say angrily:

"How dare . . you speak . . to me like . . that!"

"I think," the Baron said slowly, "you are playing 'Hard-to-get', but make no mistake, my pretty little flower, you are mine, and no one shall take you from me!"

It was then he drew her slowly towards him and Carla realised how strong he was.

She resisted him with all her strength.

But there was a smile on his thick lips as still holding

her by one hand she found it impossible not to be drawn nearer and nearer to him.

It was only when she knew that in a second she would fall against him and he would hold her to his chest and kiss her that she felt frantically that she would rather die than let him do so.

He pulled her closer still.

As she felt her feet giving way under her she reached out her hand towards the table.

Not realising what she was doing, she touched a balloon glass that was half-full of brandy.

Then with a tremendous effort as he pulled her forward she flung the contents of the glass into his face.

He gave a gutteral cry, and as he did so, released her wrist.

In that second she was free.

She flung the empty wine-glass down on the floor and ran for the door.

She pulled it open, sped down the passage and up the stairs to her bedroom.

She reached it.

Fortunately the key was in the lock as she had left it, rather carelessly when she had gone down to dinner.

She let herself in, closed the door and locked it.

Breathless and gasping, she flung herself down on the bed.

How could she have guessed, how could she have imagined that any man could behave as the Baron had done, or say such things to her?

For a moment she could only shiver.

She was horrified at what might have happened if she had not managed to escape.

It was only later when she was in bed that she thought everything over calmly.

She told herself sensibly that she had to realise that

Mr. Dessoff had brought her mother to Vienna to perform at the Opera Houe.

Therefore everything was different from her position as her father's daughter.

Now the Baron and perhaps a great number of other men would not consider her a Lady.

They would believe her to be either a paid companion to an Opera Singer, or else that she herself was indirectly connected with the stage.

Carla had travelled too much not to be aware that actresses were frowned on and ignored by Society ladies.

But it was only now that she realised what her mother was giving up so that she could earn money by her voice.

'No wonder Papa was shocked at the idea of his wife singing in public!' Carla thought bitterly.

Then she was afraid that perhaps her mother would be insulted in the same way as she had been.

'I must speak to Mr. Dessoff,' she thought, 'he will protect Mama, and I see now that it was very . . very foolish of me to go downstairs for dinner. I should have had it in my room.'

As she lay in the darkness she felt for the first time that she had grown up and would have to chaperon herself in the future.

She loathed the Baron for the way he had behaved.

At the same time, she was aware that if he had known that her mother was Lady Milbanke and she was her daughter, his conduct would have been very different.

Then she told herself that Rákó who had seemed so nice and friendly, had obviously thought the same thing.

How could he think anything else when she was sitting alone in a box in an empty Opera House without a chaperon?

"I must never see him again," she told herself.

Unexpectedly she felt she could cry at what she would be missing.

She did not sleep until it was nearly dawn.

Then she fell into a heavy slumber and dreamt she was running down a long passage.

The Baron was running after her, trying to catch her.

She awoke with a little cry and found it was quite late.

The sunshine was coming through the sides of the curtains.

She got up, put on her dressing-gown and went to her mother's room.

She listened at the door and hearing her mother talking to Anna opened it and went in.

"You are awake, Mama!" she exclaimed.

"I had a lovely long sleep," Lady Milbanke replied, "and I feel very much better and much less tired than I was yesterday."

Carla kissed her and said:

"I am glad, Mama, but now I think you should get dressed. Rehearsals are at eleven o'clock, and Mr. Dessoff is calling for you at a quarter to."

"We will have time for breakfast first," Lady Milbanke replied. "Anna has already ordered it."

She got out of bed as she spoke, then said:

"I hear you dined downstairs last night. Were you all right?"

There was just a tiny hesitation before Carla replied:

"Quite all right, Mama. I only did so because I was afraid the waiters bringing my food might waken you."

"That was sweet of you," Lady Milbanke said, "but I do not like to think that you dined alone."

"It is something I shall never do again," Carla promised.

Lady Milbanke was ready by half-past-ten.

Carla was not surprised when Mr. Dessoff arrived early.

She guessed, although he did not show it, that he too

was a little anxious in case her mother had lost her voice or was too nervous to sing.

"I am ready," Lady Milbanke said as he kissed her hand, "and I have been praying that I will not let you down."

"That is something you will not do," he smiled.

"We will go at once, so that I shall have time to draw breath before I go on stage," Lady Milbanke said.

She had already told Carla that she did not want her to go with them.

"It would make me more nervous," she said, "and whether I am a success or not, I will come back and tell you about it afterwards."

"You will be a huge success, Mama!"

Lady Milbanke turned to Anna.

"Please, Anna, get those things for me at once," she said, "especially the special spray for my throat. I managed to buy it in Paris, so I am sure they will have it in the Pharmacies here."

"I will get it at once, *Madame*," Anna promised.

Lady Milbanke kissed Carla who held her mother close to her.

"I shall be praying for you,Mama," she said, "and I know Mr. Jauner and everybody else will be astounded by your voice."

Lady Milbanke smiled at her, then she and Mr. Dessoff left.

Anna also hurried away, and Carla knew she was going to her own room to put on a bonnet and coat before she went shopping.

She debated whether she should go with her, and decided it would be something she could do later.

Then as she walked to the window to look out on to the street there was a knock at the door.

She said: "Come in!" without turning round.

She heard a page-boy say in German:

"There is a note for you, *Fräulein*."

She took it from him and when she opened it felt her heart leap!

She could hardly believe what she read.

"I have permission for us to watch Her Majesty in the Spanish Riding School this morning. If you can come with me, I am waiting outside the Hôtel in a closed carriage.

Rákó."

Carla read, then re-read it and told herself severely that it was something she must not do.

Then she knew it was an opportunity that might never come again.

The Empress might leave Vienna, in fact she was very likely to do so, as she would so much rather be in Hungary.

Alternatively Rákó, who was also Hungarian, might go away.

She would never have another chance of seeing both the Empress and the Lipizaner Riding School.

"I must go . . I must!" she said, as if she was arguing with her father.

She realised that the page-boy was waiting, and said in faltering German because she only knew very little:

"Tell the . . gentleman to wait . . for me."

He understood and hurried away, and she ran to her bedroom.

She put on her prettiest bonnet.

Instead of the fur coat she wore one which matched her gown and was close-fitting.

It was trimmed down the front and round the cuffs with fur.

She was sure it had been very expensive.

But Mr. Dessoff had instructed the Dressmakers not

to discuss the cost of anything they had brought to the house.

Carla had a quick glance in the mirror and thought her bonnet was very becoming.

"I am behaving badly!" she told her reflection, "but for the moment I am in a 'No-Man's-Land' between the Social World to which I belong and the stage, which has captured Mama."

She laughed at her fantasy and went quickly down the stairs.

She appreciated how tactful Rákó was being in not coming into the Hôtel.

If they saw him it might cause the Concierge and the porters to talk especially if he called upon her when she was alone.

The hall was full of people coming and going and she hoped nobody noticed as she slipped out through the front door.

A little way down the pavement she saw there was a closed carriage and was sure that was where Rákó would be.

He must have been looking out for her because even as she reached it, he stepped out without speaking and helped her inside.

As he joined her and the door was shut by a footman who sprang up on to the box he said:

"I was afraid you would not come."

"I knew it was . . something I should . . not do," Carla said, "but, as you said . . how can I . . resist the . . horses?"

Rákó laughed.

"That is what I was banking on, and I think it is very brave of you to join me!"

"Are you . . sure the . . Empress will be . . there?" Carla asked.

"Quite sure," he answered. "She will come at about

a quarter past eleven, and we have special permission to sit out of sight."

"How could you have got that?" Carla asked curiously.

Then before he could reply she added:

"I know the answer! They know you are Hungarian and your own horses are superb."

"That is clever of you," he said, "but you understand we must be very quiet and not talk, as the Empress does not like anyone to be there when she is riding with the Lipizaners."

As they drove on Carla said:

"Tell me about the Riding School. I only know that it is famous all over the world, and everybody talks about it."

In his deep voice, Rákó told her how the Spanish Riding School had been founded in 1572.

"It was, and is," he said, "the only place in the world in which '*Haute École*' is practised in the classical style."

"That is what I want to see!" Carla exclaimed.

"You can understand," he continued, "how much it means to the Empress, who loves horses and has taught her own a great number of tricks."

"I have heard that," Carla said, "and also that the Emperor and the Arch-Duchess disapproved of what they called 'Circus tricks'."

"That is true," Rákó agreed.

He was not smiling and he went on:

"You can understand how Her Majesty loves being in my country, where she can feel as free as the wind and she is worshipped not only for her beauty, but because she rides more brilliantly than any other woman has ever ridden before!"

Carla sighed.

"How I wish I could ride like that!"

"I would like to see you on one of my horses," Rákó

said. "But for the moment you must imagine yourself mounted on one of the 'Silver Stallions'."

Carla smiled at him.

She had no idea how lively she looked as she imagined such a thing might be possible.

They entered by a side door of the Riding School, and went up some stone steps.

When Carla saw the enormous building she felt she really had stepped into a dream.

The huge chandeliers hanging from a very high arched ceiling were lit, and the horses were already trotting round beneath them.

There were seven of them.

Their riders were all dressed in the same ancient uniform that had been passed down the centuries.

Rákó put Carla very close to one of the pillars and there was a balustrade in front of her.

They were at the back of the building, so that she knew that from the ground it would be difficult for anybody to realise they were there.

There was no one else in the place except for the horses and their riders.

Then the door at the far end with a flag on either side of it opened, and the Empress rode in.

She was riding a 'Silver Stallion'.

As the other riders saluted her Carla thought that no one could look more lovely or more elegant on a horse.

The Empress was very thin, in fact, it was said her tiny waist could be spanned by a man's two hands.

She was wearing a fashionable habit which was a dress rather than a jacket and skirt.

Carla remembered that she had read somewhere that the Empress was sewn into it every time she went riding.

It had the result that there was not a wrinkle or a fold on any part of her body.

As soon as she appeared the horses were put to a

series of exercises which they had rehearsed ever since they were four years old.

As Carla sat breathless with excitement they performed pisffes and piroettes.

They then went on to pessades, levades at high speed always in gait, and courbettes.

The Empress performed them all without a mistake or hesitation.

Finally, as Carla held her breath, the horses gave a great goat-like leap called a capriole.

Each horse started the movement on its haunches, then springing upwards, gathered its hind legs for a backward kick performed in mid-air.

It was so beautiful, so spectacular, that Carla wanted to cry out at the wonder of it.

Then she realised that without knowing she had been holding tightly on to Rákó's hand, but he was looking at her and not at the horses.

Only as the Empress, smiling and expressing her gratitude with a graceful bow, rode out of the arena, did Carla feel as if she came back to earth.

The performance was over and the seven other 'Silver Stallions' rode away.

As the last one passed through the gate Carla realised she had been holding her breath for a long time.

"That was wonderful!" she whispered.

"I thought you would think so," Rákó replied.

Slyly she took her hand from his.

They walked back the way they had come down the long passage and out of the Riding School into the sunshine.

Only then could Carla speak without whispering.

"Thank you . . thank you!" she cried. "How can I tell you how . . wonderful that was, and how . . thrilled I am . . to have seen it!"

"You wanted to see the Empress," Rákó said.

"She is . . so beautiful . . and unbelievably graceful on a horse . . that I cannot . . believe she is . . real!"

Rákó smiled.

"She is all woman – as you are!"

He spoke seriously, and Carla realised it was a compliment.

His carriage was waiting and as they stepped into it he said:

"Now you have seen one very important tradition in Vienna, I would like to take you to another."

Before Carla could say that was something she must not do, he added:

"That is to see Johann Strauss conduct and to dance to his music."

Carla gave a little gasp, then she said quickly:

"You are . . not to . . tempt me. You know it is . . hsomething I . . cannot do."

"Why not?"

She thought of what had happened last night, and had no idea how revealing her eyes were.

"There is nothing to make you afraid," Rákó said as if he could read her thoughts. "We will watch the dancing, and I will not even ask you to waltz with me, if you are afraid you might be seen."

"It is not that," Carla said, "It is just that my . . my friend . . expects me to stay in the Hotel if she is out, and anyway, when she goes to the Theatre to perform, I shall . . go with . . her."

"I understand," Rákó said. "At the same time, I shall be trying to find a time when you are unoccupied so that I can show you the real Vienna."

"That is what you have done this morning," Carla said, "and it is something I shall never forget!"

"It is very disappointing," Rákó remarked, "to read the first chapter of a book and not to find out what happens in the second!"

"Again you are tempting me," Carla protested, "and . . please . . it is . . something I must . . not do."

He was still before he said:

"You know I want to see you and all these things are only an excuse so that I can be with you, and know how incredibly lovely you are!"

For some reason she did not understand, Carla was not frightened or upset by what he was saying.

It was very different from being with the Baron last night.

As she thought of him Rákó said:

"Who has upset you? Why are you frightened?"

"I . . I do not . . want to . . talk about it."

"Tell me."

It was a plea.

At the same time, Carla felt as if it was an order, and somehow she had to obey it.

"I.it . . was the . . B.Baron," she said in a very small voice

"Baron von Erhardt?" Rákó asked. "I had heard he was staying at the Sacher Hotel, but you must have nothing to do with him!"

"I . . I could not . . help it," Carla whispered.

"What happened?"

She had no wish to tell him, but somehow her lips answered for her.

"He . . he insisted on having . . dinner with me last night in our private room!"

Rákó was frowning.

"He had no right to do such a thing and he is someone with whom you should not come in contact. You must stay away from him – do you understand?"

"He . . he frightened me," Carla said, "but . . I managed to . . escape!"

"Surely, you should not have been dining alone?"

"It was . . my own fault . . my f.friend . . was asleep,

and I thought . . if I had dinner upstairs she would be disturbed by the . . waiters."

"So you went down," Rákó finished. "It is something you are never to do again!"

He turned her round to look at her, then he said very softly:

"You are so beautiful, so unspoilt and so unsophisticated! Surely you understand that many men will find you irresistible?"

"I . . I have never been . . alone before."

"You must never be alone again!"

He put out his hand and took hers.

"Promise me," he said, "that you will not go downstairs alone in the Hotel and you will not go out into the streets alone."

His fingers tightened as he went on:

"And you are never – never! Do you understand? – to go out with another man as you have with me!"

Carla's eyes were very wide.

"Was it . . very wrong of me to . . come with you . . this morning?"

He knew she was afraid and embarrassed by what he would reply and he said quickly:

"No, of course not. This morning is different because you have seen the Empress and the horses, and it is an experience which might never come again."

"That is what I . . thought," Carla said.

"Although I will look after you and protect you," Rákó said, "other men, like the Baron, for example, may have very different ideas."

He saw the shudder that went through Carla, and the stricken expression in her eyes.

"Forget him!" he said sharply. "If he troubles you, I will deal with him. In the meantime, give me your promise that wherever you go you will have somebody with you."

"I . . promise," Carla vowed.

As she spoke the carriage came to a standstill and she realised they were outside the Sacher Hotel.

"Because I am protecting you," Rákó said, "not only from other men, but also from chattering tongues which can also be very dangerous, I will not come into the Hotel."

He took her hand as he spoke and Carla said:

"Thank you . . thank you from the . . bottom of my heart for being so . . kind."

"That is what I want to be," Rákó said, "so trust me!"

As he spoke their eyes met.

Almost as if her own voice was speaking for her, Carla heard herself say:

"I do . . trust . . you!"

CHAPTER FIVE

For the next two days Lady Milbanke was rehearsing for her aria with the Orchestra.

Mr. Dessoff arranged that she should rehearse alone early in the morning and late in the evening.

The other performers had gone home.

This was a great relief to Carla who was always afraid that her mother would become upset by other people around her.

Mr Dessoff obviously had the same idea.

He persuaded Franz Jauner that, because his *protegée* was different from anyone else she should appear only once in "*Die Walküre* and alone.

Accordingly, a scene was arranged for her at the very beginning of the Second Act.

As the 'Spirit of Valhalla' she was alone on the stage, singing of the wonders that awaited the heroes when they had died for their country.

It was a very moving aria and the music was in itself brilliant.

Combined with her mother's voice, Carla was sure it would be sensational.

Lady Milbanke also had a special white gown made for her which made her look very slim and ethereal.

In fact she looked so lovely that Mr. Dessoff told her that already the performers and workmen in the Theatre were referring to her as the 'Pocket Venus'.

There were only two days to rehearse. Then Mr. Dessoff announced that the Emperor and Empress intended to be present at the Opening Night of '*Die Walküre*'.

Carla was aware then that this was what he had secretly hoped for all the time they had been on their way to Vienna, when he had been arranging her mother's appearance.

There was no doubt that he was excited.

In fact so much so, that Carla was afraid he would make her mother nervous.

Lady Milbanke however, had met many Royalties when she had travelled with her husband.

She was therefore much more concerned with what the Viennese people in general would think rather than their reigning Sovereign.

It was as Carla was dressing to go to the Theatre that she wondered if Rákó would be there.

She did not like to admit to herself that she had missed him.

After he had taken her to the Riding School she had not heard from him or seen him again.

She found herself going over and over what she had said in the carriage.

She thought she had been so positive in saying she could not do what he suggested that he had finally given up hope of persuading her.

"Would it really . . matter," she asked herself, "if I slipped out one evening when Mama was at the Theatre, and saw Johann Strauss?"

She knew Rákó was right in that if she went home without having done so it would be something she would always regret.

The story of the '*Blue Danube*' was well-known to everybody in England.

Carla knew that to hear it conducted by Strauss himself would be very thrilling.

It seemed extraordinary now that when it was first played, it was a failure by Strauss's standards.

One *encore* was automatic for any new work by the Master, yet that was all it received at its first performance in 1867.

Strauss had been inspired to write it after reading a line from the work of Karl Isidor Beck who was the Fashionable poet at that moment.

It was he who had described the grey-green Danube which flows through Vienna as blue.

The poem would have been completely forgotten if it had not inspired Johann Strauss to compose a Waltz.

After the first performance it was just by chance that the '*Blue Danube*' was ever heard again.

In fact it was after the humiliation of the Austrians at Sadowa.

Then the country badly needed friends against Prussia and she began to woo France.

It was calculated that if the Parisiens could be enchanted by the music of Vienna, the Diplomats might find it easier to be successful.

Strauss was therefore sent to Paris on what was in reality a Diplomatic Mission.

He was fêted at a Reception at the Austrian Embassy at which the Emperor Napoleon III and Empress Eugenie were guests.

A few days later a dinner was held in his honour by a famous newspaper, the '*Figaro*'.

A Concert was arranged for Strauss and his Orchestra at the Great Reception Hall.

Strauss had become so important that he had not troubled to compose a new Waltz for the occasion.

Instead, without really discussing it with anybody, he decided to play the '*Blue Danube Waltz*, which had failed in Vienna.

The result was a wild and ecstatic ovation.

A success which actually eclipsed everything that Johann Strauss had yet achieved.

A million copies of the sheet music were sold throughout the world on the first printing.

Before he left Paris Strauss received an invitation from Edward, Prince of Wales, to come to London.

Carla had read the story a number of times.

It was always repeated and re-repeated when there was any description of a new Waltz which was inevitably compared to the '*Blue Danube*'.

When the day of the Opening of '*Die Walküre*' arrived there was no word from Rákó.

"How can I have been so stupid as not to have accepted his invitation?" she asked.

Then she told herself she was being ridiculous.

He had been kind to her, very kind, in taking her to see the Riding School.

There was however, no reason why, after she had been so adamant that she could not go anywhere else, that he should continue with his invitations.

When she thought how handsome he was.

She was sure that there were dozens if not hundreds of women waiting to do whatever he asked of them.

Therefore it was to be expected he would soon become bored with any woman who was so busy chaperoning herself that she said 'No' to everything he suggested.

She dressed herself in one of her prettiest gowns.

Then she looked in the mirror and wondered if Rákó would think her lovely, as he had said she was.

She told herself the best she could do would be to forget him.

Instead she must concentrate on her mother and pray she might soon make enough money for them to return to London.

At the same time, Carla knew that, however reprehensible it might be for Lady Milbanke to appear on the state, she was actually enjoying herself.

Nothing had been more dull or dismal than to sit in the large house in Islington wondering what they could sell.

While, because they were eating so little, they had found it an effort even to go for a walk.

Now Lady Milbanke was busy every moment.

When she was not actually rehearsing there was Mr. Dessoff who was an extremely intelligent and well read man, to talk to.

Also she had, Carla learned, made friends with Franz Jauner, who talked to her in her dressing-room.

He told her many things she wanted to know about the Opera House.

Lady Milbanke was however always concerned with Carla.

She worried in case she was bored at being so many hours of the day alone, or just sight-seeing with Anna.

"When the First Night is over, darling," she said, "I shall have more time to be with you, and Mr. Dessoff is arranging for us to go to Madrid later, which I am sure we shall both enjoy.

"I am quite happy to be here, Mama," Carla replied, "but as you say, as soon as you are freer than you are at the moment, there are so many things we can see together."

She was thinking of the Art Galleries and many of the fountains and statues in Vienna which were very beautiful.

Her Mother had not mentioned the Spanish Riding School.

Carla had however made a mental note that, if she tried to arrange to go there, she must pretend she had never been before.

Mr. Dessoff arrived at the Hotel early.

He had already told Carla he would take her to the Box which he had reserved for them both.

First, he explained, he would have to escort her mother to her dressing-room.

Now that the moment had arrived and, because she had to face a huge audience, Lady Milbanke was a little nervous.

She looked pale and as she was in her bedroom putting on a long velvet cloak in which to go to the Theatre, Carla whispered to Mr. Dessoff:

"I think you should stay with Mama until the moment she goes on stage."

He nodded his head to show he understood.

When Lady Milbanke came into the Sitting-Room he said in his usual charming manner:

"Now you look as lovely, if not lovelier than I hoped you would, and tonight you are going to make me a very proud man!"

"I . . hope I . . will not . . fail you," Lady Milbanke replied.

"You will not do that, and I feel that if I have ever done anything else in my long career, tonight I shall give to the world something that has always been missing – the music which can only have come from the spheres."

Lady Milbanke gave a little laugh, then she put her hand on Mr. Dessoff's.

"You are so kind, Gustav!" she said, "and you know that any success I may have is entirely yours."

Listening, Carla thought how clever he was to make her think of him rather than herself.

When they drove the short distance to the Opera House in Mr. Dessoff's comfortable carriage, she slipped her hand into her mother's and said:

"I am so proud of you, Mama, and I know after tonight everybody in Vienna will be talking of the 'Pocket Venus'."

Lady Milbanke laughed.

"I wonder who thought up such a ridiculous nickname!"

"That is something we shall never know," Carla said, "but I am sure the Empress will admire you because she thinks women should be slim while they say that the Emperor likes them fat."

"That is true," Mr. Dessoff said, "but the Empress eats far too little in order to keep her slim figure while your mother is sensible enough to enjoy a good meal."

Carla knew that he was very insistent that her mother should eat before she performed.

She heard him order that there should be anything she fancied, like caviar and pâté de foie gras in her dressing-room.

The one thing Carla wanted to avoid was her mother worrying what her husband had he been alive, would have thought of tonight's event.

She therefore chatted away until they reached the Opera House.

"What I am going to do," Mr. Dessoff said, "is to take you, my dear Maria, to your dressing-room, then when you are safely there, I will return to the carriage where Carla will wait for me, and take her to the Box."

"That is very sensible." Lady Milbanke agreed.

She turned to Carla.

"I hope you will be all right, my darling, and I shall think about you and Gustav when I am singing."

"I wish you Luck, dearest mama," Carla said kissing her.

Then as Mr. Dessoff helped her mother out of the carriage she sat quietly awaiting his return.

Once again she found herself thinking of Rákó and wishing he might be with her.

Surely he would know that she would be in the audience tonight?

It seemed strange that he should be so disinterested.

There had been no sign of him when she had been at the Theatre yesterday.

This morning she had sat in the Box for nearly an hour, but he had not appeared.

She had also, for which she was very grateful, not seen the Baron.

She was aware that he was still in the Hôtel.

She had been very careful never to go downstairs alone.

When she went out walking with Anna, they had gone out through a side door which prevented her from having to pass through the Reception Hall.

Quicker than she expected, Mr. Dessoff came back to the carriage.

"Come along, my dear," he said, "I will take you to the Box."

Because he had special privileges they went in through a door that was not used by the general public.

A side staircase led them to the Royal Circle without their having to use the very impressive public one.

The Auditorium was filling up and the top galleries were all packed.

Women in evening gowns were moving into the Stalls accompanied by men in white ties and tails.

Looking round, Carla saw that most of the Boxes were still empty.

The Royal Box, massed with flowers, was waiting for the Emperor and Empress.

Now the Theatre seemed to come alive.

It was very different from how it had been at rehearsals.

An air of expectation which seemed to permeate everything.

There was a number of attendants hurrying around, dressed in the smart uniform that was traditional.

Carla could see there were men in the Orchestra pit arranging the scores on the musicians' stands.

Because she thought she must think of her mother rather than herself, Carla sat down in the seat from which there was the best view of the stage.

Staring at the closed curtains she prayed that her mother would be the success that was expected and would not be frightened.

Mr. Dessoff moved restlessly about in the Box, then, as if he was nervous he said:

"I think I had better go back to your mother, my dear. You will be all right, I am sure, and I will come back before she actually sings."

"Do not worry about me," Carla said, "I am sure Mama will be happier if you are with her."

It was what Mr. Dessoff wanted to hear, and he hurried away.

When he had gone, Carla actually felt a sense of relief.

She felt she would rather be with her own thoughts.

It was difficult to make conversation when she was well aware that both shc and Mr. Dessoff could only think of her mother.

Now she realised that people were really flowing into the Theatre and the Boxes were filling up, one by one.

The ladies had certainly put on their best for the occasion.

The tiaras on their heads and the necklaces round their necks glittered and sparkled.

They seemed almost too spectacular to be anything but part of the performance.

She began to think, as only the Royal Box was empty, that perhaps the Emperor and Empress had changed their minds.

Suddenly the Orchestra, which had been playing very softly, struck up the National Anthem.

Everybody rose to their feet.

As Carla turned to look at the Royal Box she thought that nobody could look lovelier than the Empress.

Her red hair was piled on top of her head.

Her emerald tiara that was almost like a crown made her skin look translucent.

She was exquisitely lovely as she stood there holding a bouquet of orchids.

Carla found it was impossible to look at the Emperor or anybody else in the Box.

When the National Anthem ended the applause vibrated throughout the Theatre.

The Empress inclined her had and made a graceful gesture with her hand before she sat down beside her husband.

The Overture began and the light were dimmed as the curtain rose.

It was then above the noise of the music that Carla heard a deep voice behind her say:

"Are you all right alone?"

There was no need to ask who spoke and she felt her heart turn a somersault in her breast.

It took her a moment to realise that Rákó was not in the box beside her.

Instead he was in the adjoining one, sitting so close that he was almost speaking into her ear.

"Do not turn around," he said, "but go on watching the stage."

Carla did as he told her, at the same time, she was pulsatingly aware of him.

She wanted to turn her head and look into his eyes.

"Have you missed me?" he asked.

"Where have . . you been?" Carla enquired in a whisper.

"I had an appointment outside Vienna that I had to keep," he replied.

"I thought . . perhaps you had . . forgotten . . me."

She thought, although she could not see his lips, that he smiled.

"Do you really think that would be possible?" I thought of you every day, and dreamt of you every night!"

The way he spoke gave Carla sensations she had never known before.

Listening to him she was hardly aware of Wagner's music filling the air.

Nor could she take in anything that was happening on the stage.

"What have you been doing?" Rákó asked.

"Nothing very much, just sitting here during the rehearsals, and walking with a maid."

"I thought that might be happening," Rákó said, "and I knew when you were here alone that I might have been with you."

Carla did not answer and he said:

"If you are worried about your friend, I have heard already how outstanding her voice is. All Vienna is waiting to hear her."

Carla knew he was trying to prevent her from feeling anxious and she thought it was very like him to be so considerate.

"I am . . praying everything . . will be as . . you say, she replied.

"That is what I thought you were doing," he said "And have you been to the Stephansdom again?"

"Yes."

"Did you light a candle for me?"

Carla did not answer.

Actually that was what she had done, and although she told herself she was lighting it for her mother.

Yet she could not help at the same time praying that Rákó was thinking of her.

She had hoped too that it might be possible to see him again.

"You have not answered my question," he said softly.

"I . . I lit a . . candle," Carla admitted, "and I think it carried a . . prayer for . . you . . as well as the . . prayers I was saying for my . . my . . friend . . up to Heaven."

There was silence.

Then Rákó said in a different voice from the one he had used before:

"I need your prayers, Carla. I need them desperately!"

"Why?"

"That is something I cannot tell you at this moment, but if you will allow me to see you again, then I may have the opportunity."

There was silence again as Carla knew she was longing for him to ask her to meet him.

She wanted to be with him, to drive with him, anything, so long as they could be together.

She suddenly realised that somebody had come into his Box.

It was a man, and they were talking in Hungarian which was a language she did not know, so that she had no idea what they were saying.

Then she knew that, while she longed to look at Rákó, she dare not turn round.

She knew it would be a mistake so instead she sat staring at the stage.

It was only later she realised she had seen nothing.

She was in fact, surprised to find that the First Act had come to an end and Mr. Dessoff was coming into the Box.

"Your mother insisted that I came back to see if you were all right," he said, "and if there is anything you want."

"I am perfectly all right, thank you," Carla said. "How is she?"

"Very brave, and determined to be a success."

"You must go back to her at once," Carla said.

"I feel you should be with her until the very moment when she has to go on stage."

"You are a good girl," Mr. Dessoff said.

He walked towards the door and it gave Carla the excuse to get to her feet.

"Tell Mama how much I love her and how brave I think she is," she said.

"I will do that," Mr. Dessoff replied with a smile.

He went from the Box.

Now Carla could turn round and taking two steps forward could look into the next Box to see Rákó.

Then as she did so, standing up as most other people were doing, talking to each other or looking round, she realised the Box was empty.

Rákó was no longer there.

For a moment she felt as if he had deserted her.

Then she was sure that, like many of the other gentlemen he had gone down to the Bar, or perhaps was visiting other Boxes to talk to his friends.

She did not want to be noticed so she moved to the back of the Box.

She sat down in a chair where she would be out of sight.

She knew as she did so that she felt quite different from when she had first come into the Theatre.

Something seemed to have come alive within her body.

Now the music, the people, the lights and the great auditorium were all very exciting.

But what was more exciting was the fact that she had found Rákó again, or rather, he had found her.

"I wanted to see him, I wanted to talk to him," she admitted.

She knew if she was truthful that the last few days had been dull and monotonous because there had been no sign of him.

"How can I be so foolish," she asked herself. "To him I am just a 'ship that passes in the night'."

She thought he might just be amused by her because she was different.

She would not accept all his invitations and when she did they had to be surreptitious about it.

She was well aware that anyone looking as attractive as Rákó would have a great number of women in his life.

She had watched the men of many countries paying her mother compliments, kissing her hand, and looking at her with admiring eyes.

Carla was far too intelligent not to know that they would have flirted with her if Lady Milbanke had given them the slightest encouragement.

It was something they did to all the beautiful women they met.

She had watched when she had been allowed to go down to luncheon as they paid elaborate compliments.

She watched too as the women pouted their lips and looked at them provocatively from under their eye-lashes.

She knew it was the sort of game in which all young and handsome men indulged, especially the French and the Italians.

What it all came down to was that any man, whatever his nationality was attracted by a beautiful woman.

Her father had been quite right to protect her mother jealously.

He did it in a manner which made it perfectly clear to

any man who approached her that she was his and his alone.

Then she thought of the Baron and shivered.

He was the sort of man she would have to avoid and it was not only to be in Vienna.

Anywhere else that her mother's voice would carry her, she would have to be on the guard.

She could remember now how frightened she had been.

She would have to be very, very careful it never happened again.

The Interval was over and was heralded by the sound of an electric bell, and the audience came hurrying back into their seats.

Now Carla could think of nothing but her mother.

If by any terrible mischance her mother was not the success Mr. Dessoff expected, then they would return to London without being of any further importance to anyone.

Then there would be the same problems there had been before, with no hope for the future.

"Please, god, let Mama be a success!" Carla prayed.

She clenched her fingers together until they hurt.

Then as the curtain rose a deep voice behind her said:

"Do not worry, everything will be as wonderful as you are praying it will be.'

"How do . . you know I am . . frightened?" Carla asked.

"I have the same instincts you have," Rákó replied, "and I know everything will go well.'

It was then the curtains drew back.

The music softened and Carla saw for the first time the scene that Franz Jauner had designed especially for her mother.

It was very beautiful and ethereal.

It was as if it was completely insubstantial.

At the same time there were stars amongst the clouds and a sky overhead.

Then it seemed as if a figure floated rather than walked to the centre of the stage.

She too looked so insubstantial that it was impossible for her to be human.

As Lady Milbanke began to sing Carla felt as if the whole Theatre held its breath.

Her voice was so pure, so clear, that it was difficult to believe it came from a human person.

Instead she was in fact what she portrayed, the 'Spirit of Valhalla'.

She was telling the heroes who had died there was no such thing as death, only Life Everlasting.

It was a lovely aria in itself, but Carla knew that her mother's voice made it special, something different from what anyone had ever heard.

It was, as Mr. Dessoff believed, the voice of an angel.

As she sang her voice seemed to rise higher and higher, until she touched notes that had never been heard before.

Then just as she had appeared through the white clouds, they enveloped her, and she vanished.

For several seconds there was the greatest accolade of all – complete silence.

Then the cheers broke out and the audience rose spontaneously to its feet.

It was a reception that was unparalleled even in the history of many great ovations in the Viennese Theatre.

Then because Franz Jauner was a great Showman, to everybody's astonishment the singer did not reappear.

Instead, the scene became transformed into the usual Second Act of '*Die Walküre*'.

There was Brünnhilde singing the familiar arias to Siegmund, but without the magic that Lady Milbanke had brought to the Opera.

While everybody stood and cheered, Carla had not moved.

She had merely sat still in her chair unaware that the tears had run down her cheeks.

Now as everybody seated themselves again and the Show continued, she heard Rákó say very quietly:

"That was beautiful! As beautiful as you are!"

With an effort Carla wiped her eyes and he said:

"Now that you have no need to be worried or frightened you can think about me."

She gave a little murmur and he said:

"I have an idea and tomorrow I will send you a message. It will come with some flowers which remind me of you."

As he finished speaking she heard the door of the box open and Mr. Dessoff joined her.

As he sat down beside her, Carla knew by the expression on his face how contented he was, and how thrilled by her mother's success.

"She is all right?" she asked.

"Marvellous!" he replied, "but she wanted to go back to the Hotel."

"Go back?" Carla repeated. "But surely, she will have to appear at the end?"

Mr. Dessoff shook his head.

"Jauner and I thought it out between us, that tonight when everybody is expecting her, they will be disappointed. There will be a great 'hue and cry' because she is not there to take the bouquets and the applause that will be waiting for her."

For a moment Carla just stared at him, then she gave a little laugh.

"I can see how that will intrigue everybody," she said, "so that they will all come to the Theatre again and again, until they do see her!"

"Exactly!" Mr. Dessoff replied, "and because your

mother is different from the average performer, they will resent her missing the Finale, which is another way of her being unique."

Carla rose to her feet.

"Then let us leave," she said.

They walked out of the Box and down the side staircase which brought them to the door by which they had entered.

Mr. Dessoff's carriage was waiting, and having helped Carla into it, he went to fetch her mother.

Wrapped in the long velvet cloak which covered her, a chiffon scarf over her heard, Lady Milbanke hurried across the pavement and into the waiting carriage.

She sat down beside Carla.

"You were fantastic, Mama!" Carla said.

"There is no other word to describe it!" Mr. Dessoff added, taking the seat opposite her. "You are quite certain, my dear Maria, that you do not mind leaving before the Finale?"

"No, I am so relieved and happy that I can go now," Lady Milbanke said.

They drove the short way to the Hôtel.

In their Suite Mr. Dessoff was supervising the supper he had ordered while Carla went into her mother's bedroom with her.

"You were so wonderful, Mama," she said, "and I could hardly believe it was you!"

"Because it was so difficult to see through the mist they created and because the lights were in my eyes,' Lady Milbanke said, "I could hardly see the audience and I forgot they were there. I thought I was singing to you, dearest, when you were a little girl, and after that it was easy."

Carla put her arms round her mother and hugged her.

"I never imagined any audience could applaud with such vigour. The men were all on their feet, shouting and waving, and they made more noise than anything Wagner could compose!"

Lady Milbanke laughed.

She had taken off her cloak and laid it on the bed, and now she was tidying her hair in the mirror.

"It was such fun," she said, "that we could creep away like this, and if there are any bouquets for me, they can be sent here so that we can look at them without feeling Brünnhilde or any of the other performers are wanting to deprive me of them!"

As she spoke she went into the Sitting-Room.

Mr. Dessoff rose to his feet and handed her a glass of champagne.

"No one," he said, "is going to believe, watching the Second Act, that this is happening."

"But it is!" Lady Milbanke said, "and I was just saying to Carla how happy I am to be here with you alone."

"You realise," Mr. Dessoff said, "they will be calling for you?"

"If they want me as much as all that," Lady Milbanke said, "they will have to come back tomorrow night to see me."

"I think it was a very clever idea," Carla said, "and anyway, it would be a mistake for Mama to be seen too closely by anyone in the audience, just in case they recognise her."

Lady Milbanke gave a little cry.

"I never thought of that!"

"It need not worry you," Mr. Dessoff said quickly, "you look so different wearing theatrical make-up, and even your hair was covered."

"Yes, of course," Lady Milbanke said, "but I hope tomorrow night and every other night I shall go on escaping."

"We will talk about it with Jauner," Mr. Dessoff

promised. "Now enjoy yourself. I know you are hungry."

"I think, really, I am too excited to eat," Lady Milbanke said, "but I expect you are thinking more of my voice than of me, so I will try to eat, like a human being."

It was certainly a delicious supper.

Carla found herself laughing at the things Mr. Dessoff had told them were happening backstage.

This included the fact that one of the horses had managed to eat most of the oats that had been provided for Brünnhilde's horse.

They had to send out for another supply.

"I really wanted to see the '*Ride of the Valkyries*' tonight," Carla confessed. "It was such a muddle at the final rehearsal that I can hardly believe it went off without something going wrong."

"You shall watch it tomorrow," Mrs. Dessoff said reassuringly.

As soon as supper was finished, he insisted that Lady Milbanke should go to bed.

"Whatever you may say," he said, "it has been a great strain, and personally, I feel exhausted!"

"We will go to bed as you tell us to do," Lady Milbanke said, "and thank goodness, tomorrow I need not get up early for rehearsals."

"You can stay in bed and sleep until luncheontime," Mr. Dessoff said. "I am sure you will have dozens of invitations, but I hope you will both have luncheon with me."

"Of course," Lady Milbanke agreed.

Only when she reached her own room was Carla able to think of Rákó.

It gave her a warm feeling in her heart that he had come back and that he had promised to send her another invitation.

She only hoped it was one she could accept.

Then even as she thought of him she knew that however difficult it might be, however much her conscience might prick her, she would do what Rákó asked.

Without him there was something missing.

She did not want to put what it was into words.

She only knew that her heart was singing because he was thinking of her.

CHAPTER SIX

"If you receive any more flowers," Carla exclaimed, "there will be no room for us!"

The bouquets for her mother had been arriving since first thing in the morning.

The whole of the large Sitting-Room was now filled with them.

There were flowers of every sort and description and a great many of them were the most expensive orchids.

Carla could not help thinking that even one bunch of them in London would have kept them in food for a week.

At the same time, it was thrilling for lady Milbanke to realise what a success she had been.

Anna had gone out early to buy newspapers and every one of them had a description of last evening in headlines.

Needless to say the Journalists had learnt that she had already been nicknamed the 'Pocket Venus', and had made use of it in their columns.

Carla sat on her Mother's bed trying to read the newspapers.

But almost every minute she had to go into the Sitting-Room to decide where new flowers which had just arrived should be put.

Finally she brought two vases into the bedroom and placed them on either sidc of her mother.

"They smell delicious!" she said, "and they make you look as if you are sitting in a Fairy bower!"

"I feel that is where I am," Lady Milbanke replied, "but it is only a dream, and I shall wake up to find myself in Islington, wondering what I can sell."

"I think that is something which will never happen again," Carla said.

At the same time, she could not help wondering what the future held.

At her age her mother could hardly wander around Europe for many years singing at the different Opera Houses.

Although Lady Milbanke did not realise it at the moment, she would find it difficult to be permanently surrounded by Theatrical people.

With them, however nice they were, she had little in common.

But those were problems which Carla did not want to think about at the moment, even though they kept recurring in her mind.

Mr. Dessoff arrived before luncheon and was even more excited than they were.

"I have been congratulated by everybody!" he said, "until I feel like a man who has discovered the source of the Nile or reached the North Pole!"

"I do not feel like an icicle at the moment," Lady Milbanke protested, "in fact I am so happy that I have not failed you, and that I have justified your faith in me."

"Only you could say anything so kind," Mr. Dessoff replied, "but it is your triumph, and you are now acclaimed as the greatest soprano of our time!"

Lady Milbanke looked a little embarrassed and he went on:

"As you can imagine, the Journalists of every newspaper are clamouring for an interview with you. What am I to tell them?"

Lady Milbanke gave a cry of horror.

"Oh . . please . . I do not wish to see them . . and you know if they asked me about . . my life before I came to Vienna . . it would be very . . difficult to know . . what to . . say."

"I have thought of that," Mr. Dessoff said, "and I think you should remain an enigma as you were last night. It will give them something to write about, but you must be prepared to be besieged whenever you leave the building."

"We could slip out through a back door," Carla suggested, knowing that was what she had been doing because of the Baron.

"I thought of that," Mr. Dessoff smiled, "and we will manage to avoid them somehow. At any rate, for the moment."

They had luncheon in their private room.

Afterwards Mr. Dessoff said that Lady Milbanke had to return to the Opera House in order for them to make a few adjustments to the lights.

"We will not be there for long," he explained, "so there will be no need for Carla to come, if she wishes to do anything else."

Carla looked out of the window.

It was a dismal day with no sun, and the dark clouds in the sky promised rain.

"If I stay here," she said, "I can pretend I am in a sunlit garden with flowers growing all around me."

"The only difficulty is," Lady Milbanke laughed, "is where you are to sit."

"The next lot of flowers will go into your bedroom," Carla said, "and after that they will be in mine."

She helped her mother dress, then Mr. Dessoff took her downstairs, and out by the kitchen door.

He had already ascertained it was free from Journalists at the moment.

Carla did not go down with them because she was frightened of meeting the Baron.

Instead, she re-arranged the flowers, wondering when those which Rákó had promised her would arrive.

She was half-afraid they had already done so and she had thought they were for her mother.

Most of those had a label or a card inscribed:

"To the Pocket Venus." "To the Angel with the Golden Voice."

She was reading the newspapers when her mother returned, and she realised she had been away not more than an hour.

"We drove past the front of the Hôtel," Lady Milbanke told her, "and there was a huge crowd there, not only Journalists with cameras, but also a number of the public with autograph-books."

"It is the biggest crowd I have ever seen for a Prima Donna," Mr. Dessoff said with satisfaction.

"My dressing-room at the Opera house was also filled with flowers," Lady Milbanke smiled.

"They must all have cost a lot of money!" Carla said.

She met her mother's eyes and knew that she was thinking the same thing she had thought this morning.

When they had sold their treasures and their clothes the money they had received for them was a mere 'drop in the ocean' compared to what was beong expended on her mother's voice.

'I suppose really,' Carla thought, 'we never appreciated how wonderful it was, and certainly never thought of exploiting it as we might have done.'

Now everything was changed.

As Lady Milbanke was getting ready to go to the Theatre she thought how fantastic it was to have a mother who could take the whole Music World by storm.

"And here am I," she told herself mockingly, "unable to earn a penny!"

She suddenly remembered what the Baron had offered her and felt not only disgusted, but humiliated.

Mr. Dessoff had as usual ordered Lady Milbanke something light to eat before they left for the Opera House.

He arrived just when the table had been laid and the waiter was opening a bottle of wine.

"I have tremendous news!" he said excitedly as he came in through the door.

"What is it?" Carla asked.

"His Majesty the Emperor has requested that your mother sings after a dinner-party he is giving at the Palace tomorrow night!"

For a moment neither Carla nor Lady Milbanke spoke.

Then Carla said:

"Have you accepted for Mama to go?"

"How could I do anything else but inform His Majesty that it was a great honour?" Mr. Dessoff replied.

"But . . how can I appear at . . the Opera House and . . the Palace?" Lady Milbanke asked.

"Very easily," Mr. Dessoff answered. "As soon as you have sung before Act II we drive to the Palace and I have calculated they will only just have left the dinner-table."

Carla gave a little cry.

"But . . Mama, it will be so exciting for you! Think of actually meeting the Empress and talking to her! You could not see how lovely she looked last night."

"I suppose I had better change at the Opera House," Lady Milbanke said in a practical tone, "and my Dresser can re-arrange my hair after I have cleaned the grease-paint off my face."

"Of course! Of course!" Mr. Dessoff agreed.

Carla thought with amusement that he was more thrilled at the idea of them going to the Palace than her mother was.

She knew it was because she had been to so many Royal Palaces with her father, including Buckingham Palace.

Now she was more concerned with the practical side of going there than the honour and the glory.

"There is no chance, I suppose, of Carla coming too?" Lady Milbanke asked.

"I am afraid not," Mr. Dessoff said, "and, quite frankly, my dear, it would be a mistake. We do not want anyone to suspect that she is your daughter."

"No, I suppose not," Lady Milbanke sighed, "but I would like her to have seen the inside of the Schönbrunn which I understand is very impressive."

"You will be able to tell her all about it when you come home, which I imagine will be quite late."

Lady Milbanke looked at him enquiringly and he explained:

"Royal dinner-parties are very long-drawn-out, and no one can leave until the Emperor and the Empress retire. If they are amused, the party can often go on into the early hours of the morning."

"Mama must not be over-tired," Carla said quickly.

'No, of course not," Mr. Dessoff agreed, "but she can stay in bed the following day. There is no need for her to rehearse as she is already perfect in her part."

"That is what I want to hear," Lady Milbanke said.

They set off to the Opera House and Carla was wondering if Rákó would again be in the next Box.

When she arrived it was to find the Box was occupied by a party of people chatting to each other in German.

She felt instinctively that they were not friends of Rákó's.

The Opera House seemed fuller than it had the night before.

She knew it was due to the publicity about her mother in the newspapers.

There was also a very enthusiastic audience who were by no means as formal as they had been the previous night.

They clapped at everything, and after her mother had sung to complete silence, the ovation was even louder and wilder than it had been before.

As she vanished into the clouds and the Act II started the audience refused to settle down and accept the fact that the 'Pocket Venus' had gone.

They stood up in the Auditorium shouting for her.

They made so much noise that they drowned the music, and the people on the stage were not certain how to proceed.

Finally the curtain came down and Franz Jauner came onto the stage to remonstrate with them.

"It is quite useless to demand to see the 'Spirit of Valhalla'," he said. "She has returned to where she came from!"

He paused, then he said:

"Of course, you can always join her there!"

This was a joke at which almost reluctantly the audience laughed.

Then, when he had promised that they would see the 'Pocket Venus' tomorrow night, he left the stage.

The second act started again.

Driving back to the Hôtel, Lady Milbanke said:

"I feel as if slipping away like this I am rather cheating the people who pay to see me."

"I have already discussed that with Jauner," Mr. Dessoff said. "He has decided, with your permission, that when '*Die Walküre*' ends in eight days time – he has arranged for ten performances – you shall appear in the *Finale* on the last night."

"I think I shall be rather nervous," Lady Milbanke said.

She paused for a moment before she asked:

"What happens to me after that?"

"We have not yet decided," Mr. Dessoff replied. "If you were an ordinary *Prime Donna* you would of course have been given a part in '*Aida*' or '*Lohengrin*' with which I intend shall follow this one."

"I am sure you are thinking that for Mama it would be an anti-climax!' Carla intervened.

"You are quite right, Carla," Mr. Dessoff agreed. "That is exactly what I have been saying, but for the moment no decision has been made, and we are all thinking about it very seriously."

He took them up to their Suite at the Hôtel, then left saying to Carla:

"I think your mother should go to bed. There has been a lot of excitement today, and tomorrow there will be the visit to the Palace. She must rest."

"Yes, of course," Carla agreed.

"You are a very sensible girl," Mr. Dessoff said.

When he had gone Carla helped her mother into bed, then went to her own room.

She was feeling suddenly very dismal because she had not seen Rákó at the Theatre, and there were no flowers.

Then as she stood at the window looking out at the lighted streets and wondering what he was doing, there was a knock on her door.

She unlocked it and found a page-boy outside, holding a bouquet in his hand.

"This has just arrived for you, *Fräulein*," he said, "with instructions not to bring it upstairs until you had retired to bed."

Carla took the flowers from him and when the boy had gone she looked at them.

They were a bunch of very small white lilies not yet in bloom.

She knew why Rákó had chosen them and felt herself blush.

Tucked into the very centre of the bouquet she found what she was seeking.

It was a small note without an envelope hidden unless one was looking for it amongst the flowers.

She unfolded the note and read:

"Tomorrow night, when you are alone, I shall be waiting to take you to hear Johann Strauss himself.

Rákó."

Carla read and re-read the note.

She knew without him saying so that he was aware her mother was going to the Palace.

It was therefore a perfect opportunity.

He could take her, as he wished to do, to hear the Master who had contributed more than anyone else to the music of Vienna.

"How can I possibly refuse?" she asked herself.

Then as she held the lilies against her breast, she knew that no pangs of conscience, no sense of propriety, would prevent her from going with Rákó tomorrow night.

She could be counting the hours until she could do so.

As she got into bed she found herself thinking of how exciting it was that she had met him.

Although he was a complete stranger, she felt as if she had known him all her life.

She did not ask why she felt like that.

She only knew that she trusted Rákó just as she had

known from the first moment she met the Baron that she could not trust him.

He was crude, unpleasant, and even in a way wicked, while Rákó was the complete opposite.

"I trust . . him!" she whispered, "and I know he would . . never hurt or . . humiliate me."

At the same time, she thought it strange that she knew so little about him.

In fact only his Christian name, and that he was Hungarian.

There was something dashing and virile about him, she thought, which she had always associated with the Hungarians.

The Germans were stolid, aggressive and, like the Baron, often menacing.

The Hungarians were romantic, perhaps wild, but at the same time, inspiring.

"I suppose I am being ridiculous about the only two young men I have talked to since I grew up," Carla tried to say.

She was sure however, that she was not unique in thinking that Rákó was different.

But perhaps what she felt was just part of the Fairy-Story of Vienna.

When they left she would never see him again although he would always be in her memory.

Because he was so handsome she could compare him with everyone she met.

In which case, she might never fall in love.

It was then she tried deliberately not to go on thinking about Rákó and to try to go to sleep.

Yet, she could almost hear his deep voice talking to her.

She could also feel the sensations he aroused in her when he touched her hand.

Sensations that were very different from what she had ever felt before.

"I am feeling like this because I am in Vienna," she told herself desperately.

Then she acknowledged that was not true.

. . . .

Both Lady Milbanke and Carla slept late the following morning: in Carla's case because she had not slept until nearly dawn.

As she drew back the curtains, the sun was shining and the sky was no longer overcast.

Also it was much warmer than it had been yesterday. In fact, she told herself, Spring had gone.

It was difficult to think of anything else when she went into the Sitting Room.

She was almost over-powered by the fragrance of the flowers and the beauty of them.

Because they were so late they had breakfast in her mother's bedroom.

Carla sat planning which gown Lady Milbanke would wear at the Palace and what flowers would look best in her hair as she had no tiara.

"I wish I had not sold the diamond tiara your father gave me," Lady Milbanke said a little wistfully, "or my necklace of pearls and diamonds which was so beautiful and always greatly admired."

"We have enough exquisite orchids to make you look like a Princess, Mama," Carla said, "and if you wear one on a piece of velvet round your neck, you will at least look different from all the other ladies."

"That is a good idea," Lady Milbanke agreed. "At the same time, I shall feel slightly undressed, knowing how much they will all glitter including the Empress."

There was nothing they could do about that, Carla thought.

Then, just before it was time for luncheon, a page-boy came upstairs with a parcel.

"It looks like a book!" Carla said before her mother undid it, "and that at least will be a change from flowers!"

She picked up the paper in which the parcel had been wrapped.

As she was throwing it into the waste-paper basket she heard her mother gasp.

She turned round and saw that what had arrived was not a book, but a velvet box.

Her mother had opened it and inside was a diamond necklace.

"Mama!" Carla exclaimed. "Who could have sent you that?"

"I have no idea," her mother replied, "and of course it is something I cannot accept."

"Of course not," Carla agreed, "but who sent it?"

As she spoke she retrieved the piece of paper which had been attached to the top of the box and which had fallen off when Lady Milbanke opened it.

On it, written in Italian, were the words:

"To the Angel whose voice carried me through the Gates of Heaven!"

There was no signature.

Carla turned the piece of paper over to look at the back and also retrieved the covering she had thrown into the basket.

But there was nothing to indicate who the giver might be.

"How is it possible," Lady Milbanke asked, "that

anybody should spend so much money without expecting to be thanked for it?"

"At least it solves the problem of what you should wear tonight, Mama," Carla smiled.

"I do not feel I should wear it," Lady Milbanke said in a shocked voice. "How could I do such a thing when I have no idea who has given it to me?"

"You mean to leave it here in its box?" Carla asked. "It seems a pity."

They were talking about the diamond necklace all the afternoon.

Finally when they packed Lady Milbanke's gown to take with her to the Theatre, the necklace went with it.

"Perhaps somebody in the Palace will identify himself," Carla suggested, "in which case you can say 'Thank you very much!' then give it back."

"Yes, of course, I shall do that," Lady Milbanke agreed, "but I know my gown will look much better if I wear it."

The same procedure took place as the two previous nights.

Carla was taken to the Box and Mr. Dessoff stayed with her mother until just before she was due to sing.

Her performance was followed by an ovation which held up the Opera for nearly ten minutes.

"The one person who is delighted with all this, is Jauner," Mr. Dessoff said. "Every seat in the Theatre is sold out until '*Die Walküre*' ends."

He did not wait for Carla to reply, but hurried away to be with her mother.

He had to prevent her from being interrupted in her dressing-room, when she had to change into the gown she was to wear at the Palace.

In the meantime, on his instructions, Carla was taken down to the carriage, and she waited until her mother and Mr. Dessoff joined her.

Before they dropped her off at the Hôtel, she was able to see how lovely Lady Milbanke looked.

She was wearing a gown which was of silver and very pale grey tulle, and she looked almost as ethereal as she did on stage.

The diamond necklace glittered round her neck

At the back of her head were just a few of the small star-like orchids which some Admirer had sent to her.

Carla knew without him saying so how proud Mr. Dessoff was to be escorting her.

He was also delighted at being able to present her Mother to the Emperor and Empress.

She noticed, although she did not say anything, that he wore several decorations on his evening-coat, and a cross on a red ribbon round his neck.

There was no doubt he was a very distinguished man.

Carla could understand that, because he had done so much for the Music World, he had a special place in Viennese Society.

The carriage stopped at the side entrance to the Sacher Hôtel.

In the front there would be a large number of Journalists and autograph-hunters, hoping against hope they would see the 'Pocket Venus'.

Carla kissed her mother goodnight and hurried through the side door and up the staircase which took her to the First Floor.

There was no one in the Suite.

She had told Anna not to wait up as she would not require any assistance when she put herself to bed.

Anna had a great number of friends in Vienna, and when she was not on duty, she spent her time with them.

Carla tidied her hair in the mirror, well aware that her heart was beating quickly.

When she went downstairs there was just one dangerous moment when she had to pass through the hall and out through the main entrance.

She knew however, that she would not be recognised.

Seeing one of the young porters on duty she asked him if he would take her out to a carriage that was waiting for her.

She kept her head down as she pushed through the crowds who were chatting amongst themelves.

They were also watching the roadway for anyone approaching the hotel rather than leaving it.

Rákó's carriage was exactly where it had been when he had collected her before.

Climbing out of the carriage, he tipped the porter who had escorted her before he joined her inside.

Then as the horses started off he said:

"I knew you would be brave enough to come, but I was afraid something might stop you."

"The . . temptation of seeing . . Johann Strauss was too . . strong!" Carla replied.

"I thought it would be," Rákó said, "and you will understand that now he is getting old he only occasionally conducts the Orchestra himself."

"And that is what he is doing tonight?" Carla asked eagerly.

"He is, and it is rather a special occasion," Rákó replied.

"Tell me why," Carla pleaded.

"A distinguished Viennese family have taken over one of the Dance Halls in order to celebrate their son's twenty-first birthday."

Carla was listening excitedly.

She had heard of the Viennese Dance Halls and Anna had told her about them, but she had never expected to see one.

She had a feeling that as Rákó was talking he had something very special to say to her.

"You will understand," he said, "that if I had said I was bringing you – a friend of the 'Pocket Venus' – you would invite a great deal of curiosity."

"Yes, of course," Carla agreed, "and that is . . something I do not . . want."

"On the other hand, if I just said you were a friend of mine," Rákó went on, "there would be just as much curiosity – but it would be a little different."

Carla knew exactly what he meant.

She was well aware she could not appear in London alone with a young man to whom she was not officially engaged.

If she did the Social Hostesses would be very inquisitive as to who she was, and why Rákó was with her.

"I therefore said I was bringing to the party a distant cousin of mine," Rákó went on, "who has never been to Vienna before, but had her parents' permission to be with me tonight."

Carla looked at him in surprise, then realised he was smiling.

"Because they think you are 'playing truant', everything has been arranged. We will not be received by the Host and Hostess, but will slip into the Hall and sit quietly in one of the small alcoves where we are unlikely to be disturbed.

Carla clapped her hands together.

"How can you think of . . anything so . . clever!" she exclaimed.

"You must realise that I would not take you to an ordinary Dance Hall," Rákó continued, "which can at times be very noisy and you might be insulted by men who would want to dance with you because you are so beautiful."

Carla drew in her breath thinking that was something which would frighten her.

"As it is," Rákó said, "we can listen to Johann Strauss

until it is time for you to go back to the Hôtel, and I shall have shown you again something of the real Veinna."

"Thank you . . thank you," Carla said. "You are . . so kind. I . . understand exactly what . . you are . . saying . . and I know I . . need not be . . nervous."

"It is something I have no wish for you to be," Rákó said in a caressing tone, "and you know I will protect you."

She had a feeling as he spoke that he was thinking of the Baron and of men like him.

She repressed an impulse to move a little closer to him.

When they reached the Dance Hall she saw it was a large building in one of the brightly lit streets.

There was a number of smart carriages standing outside it.

They did not go through the main door, but Rákó took her round the building to a side antrance.

Carla thought a little mockingly that she was continually looking for side entrances in one place or another.

She did not say anything.

The servants who opened the door took them down a passage which was poorly furnished and uncarpeted.

Then as Rákó opened a door there was the sound of music.

She found herself in an alcove which was not unlike a Box at the Theatre.

It had curtains on each side of it, and a table laid for two.

As they sat down Carla realised they could see the dance-floor while they themselves, half-hidden by the curtains, were almost invisible.

Then she could think of nothing but the Orchestra which she could see was on the balcony above the floor at the end of the Hall.

At the moment there was no Conductor, and the music was soft and romantic.

The Hall itself had an arched roof painted a pale blue and picked out in gold leaf.

There were alcoves rather like their own all round the Dance Floor.

A balcony on the same level as the Orchestra was packed with people standing watching the dancing and going down various staircases to join in.

The lights were dazzling, and there was a profusion of flowers.

Carla knew because it was a private party that the Ladies were better-dressed and, like the gentlemen, were distinguished.

A waiter brought them wine and put plates containing a delectable variety of *petit fours* on the table.

Carla, however, was watching the dancing.

Only when she was aware that Rákó was watching her, did she smile at him a little shyly.

He bent forward to say something to her, then at that moment the music stopped.

Those who had been dancing came to a standstill and burst into spontaneous applause.

A man had appeared on the balcony who Carla knew was Johann Strauss.

He was not as good-looking as she had expected, but he undoubtedly had a presence which she could sense even at a distance.

She had heard a great deal about him from Anna who was an ardent admirer.

The maid told her somewhat indiscreetly that he had a morbid fear of old age.

He therefore constantly surrounded himself with young girls, believing they would recreate his youth.

Anna also said he dyed his greying hair, and it certainly appeared untouched by age, and was a very deep red.

He bowed to those on the Dance Floor.

Then, turning to the Orchestra, raised his baton and the Orchestra began a spirited Waltz.

The guests piled onto the floor, swinging round laughing as they did so.

They created a picture that seemed to Carla to be one of joy and happiness.

She knew as she listened that the music under Johann Strauss' baton was more alive than she could have ever expected any music could be.

She realised that it was Strauss' genius that he could infuse his own vitality into sounds which beguiled the world and enchanted those who listened to it.

"This was what you wanted to hear," Rákó said.

"It is . . very . . very romantic!" she said.

"This is what I think," he replied, "but not because of the music, but because you are here with me."

He was speaking very seriously, and his voice seemed to be deeper than usual.

For a moment, Carla felt as if they were alone on an island.

There was no one near them, except for the music which came from the sky, the sea, and perhaps from the palm-trees above them.

She realised because his eyes were looking into hers that it was impossible to look away and he could read her thoughts.

Then he said very softly:

"That is where I long to be with you, and I think we should be very happy."

She felt herself quiver.

It was almost as if he was touching her and she was in his arms.

Then he said:

"I love you! Of course I love you, and you must be aware of it!"

"You . . love . . me?" Carla stammered.

"How can I help it," he asked, "when you are the most beautiful person I have ever seen, and everything about you is perfect!"

He drew in his breath before he went on:

"I adore you because you are so unspoiled, so unself-conscious! I love your shyness, and the way you try to protect yourself agsinst me!"

Carla could not breathe.

She could only look at him, her eyes very wide, and know little thrills were running through her body like starlight.

"How can you be so incredibly lovely?" Rákó asked, "and how can I do anything but lay my heart at your feet?"

It was impossible for Carla to answer him.

She felt as if he swept her up into the sky and she was so happy she knew she must be in a dream.

Then suddenly the lights in the Hall were dimmed and very softly Strauss began the first notes of his '*Blue Danube*'.

It was then Rákó put out his hand, and taking Carla from her seat went from their alcove onto the Dance Floor.

He held her very close against him.

Then they were moving slowly and so perfectly attuned to each other that they might have been one person.

Every note spoke to Carla in Rákó's voice.

She felt the melody move through her body as it moved through his, and they were indivisible.

They went round and round the floor, and she was conscious of the strength of his arms, and the closeness of him.

She thought too, that once or twice his lips touched her hair.

Then as he knew the music was coming to an end, Rákó stepped with her from the Dance Floor and took her back to their alcove.

He did not speak to her or say what they were going to do.

He merely took her wrap from the chair where she had laid it and placed it round her shoulders.

Then they were walking out of the alcove and down the passage through which they had come.

The music became fainter and fainter, until, as they reached the door into the street they could hear it no longer.

Rákó's carriage was waiting for them.

He helped her into it, gave some instructions to the footman who had opened the door, and they drove off.

As they did so, Carla turned towards him and the next second she was in his arms.

He held her against him and his lips were on hers.

He kissed her passionately, demandingly, possessively until she felt she was no longer herself, but a part of him.

She then found she was feeling an ecstasy that was so intense, so wonderful that it was almost impossible to think.

She could only feel, and go on feeling until, as if she broke under the strain of such rapture, she hid her face against his neck.

"My darling, my sweet!" he exclaimed, and his voice was very unsteady.

Then as if he could not let her go he turned her face up to his and was kissing her again.

It was only after what seemed a century of rapture that Carla realised the horses had come to a standstill.

She thought they must be back at the Hôtel.

Then when she looked out through the window, she knew they had stopped at one of the huge fountains that was playing in an open Park.

The great stream of water jetted up into the starlit sky was very lovely.

For a moment she could only stare at it until Rákó drew her back against him.

Then he was kissing her passionately until they were both breathless.

Because the intensity of her feelings almost overcame her, she put up her hand as if in defence.

He raised his head and looked at her.

"My precious heart," he said, "I am not frightening you?"

"I . . love you," Carla whispered. "I love you . . until there is . . nothing in the . . whole world but . . you."

"My sweet, my darling, it is what I have wanted you to say," Rákó replied, "but this is something which should not have happened."

Carla did not understand.

As she looked at him enquiringly he could see her face clearly by the light which illuminated the base of the fountain.

Then he said:

"I have brought you here, my darling, to say goodbye, and God knows how I can let you go!"

"T. to . . say . . goodbye?"

It was then she felt as if a cold hand clutched at her heart.

CHAPTER SEVEN

For a moment Carla could only stare at Rákó.

She felt that something terrible was happening, yet she did not know what it was.

Then as if he did not trust himself to be near to her Rákó moved across the carriage.

He sat down on the small seat, with his back to the horses, facing her.

They could see each other very clearly in the light from the fountain.

Because the water was falling iridescent from the sky into the sculpted bowl beneath it everything to Carla seemed unreal.

She felt as if suddenly she had stepped into a nightmare.

Then surprisingly Rákó reached out to take her gloved hand in his.

He very gently unbuttoned and drew off her long white kid glove.

She had worn gloves when she was dancing.

When he had taken her from the Dance Hall into the carriage she had slipped off the left-hand glove before he had begun to kiss her.

After that she had forgotten everything but the rapture his lips gave her.

Now, as she stared at Rákó, he held her hand in both of his to look down at it before he kissed the softness of her skin.

She felt herself quiver at the insistence of his lips.

Then he took her other hand and kissed that too, before holding them both in his as he said:

"I must try to explain to you, my precious, and I must not kiss your lips again or else it will be impossible to leave you as I have to do!"

"But . . why . . why?" Carla asked.

"That is what I am going to tell you," he replied. "And it is the most difficult thing I have ever had to do in my whole life!"

"I . . I do not . . understand!' Carla whispered

Rákó drew a deep breath. Then he said:

"It has been so wonderful in our Dream World into which we stepped when we first talked together, and you have never asked me any curious questions."

Carla did not speak, but her eyes were on his.

She could hear the pain in his voice as he said:

"You were right when you remembered that my name was the same as Prince Rákóczi, one of the great romantic heroes of Hungary."

Carla looked puzzled and Rákó said quietly:

"I am his direct descendant! I am the present Prince Rákóczi, the Head of the family that has existed for hundreds of years!"

Carla gave a little murmur and would have taken her hands from his.

But he held on to them, holding them so tightly that it was painful.

"Because I am who I am," Rákó said harshly, "I have to marry – someone of whom my family will approve – someone they will consider their – equal!"

He said the words as if they were forced from his lips.

Then, in a very different tone of voice he said:

"How can I explain to you – how can I make you understand that Rákóczi family would never accept the daughter of a singer, however beautiful and unusual she might be."

Carla drew in her breath.

"The . . daughter?" she stammered.

"I suspected that you were Maria Ravello's daughter," Rákó said, "even before I heard you in the Box talking to Mr. Dessoff."

"Mama did not . . want people to . . know who I was . . in case I . . would be . . associated with her and . . and she was . . protecting me."

"She is right – completely right!" Rákó said, "but if we were married, my darling, which I want more than life itself, my family would snub or ignore you, and however much I tried I could not prevent you from being hurt and unhappy."

He looked down at her hands as he said:

"Why in God's name does this have to happen to me? You have stolen my heart, and I will never – and this is a vow, Carla – love anybody else again!"

He raised her hands to his lips and kissed them one after the other passionately.

Then he asked in an agonising manner:

"Why do we torture ourselves? There is nothing I can do but leave Vienna at once."

As he spoke he released her hands with a gesture which seemed to throw them from him.

He opened the door and half-stepped out to say to the servant sitting on the box:

"Drive to the Hôtel."

As he shut the door and the horses started off, Carla said in a broken little tone:

"I . . I . . love y.you!"

"As I love you!" Rákó said savagely, "but you must forget me."

"How . . can I do . . that?"

"You are very beautiful," he said, "and you will find a man who will make you a good husband, and protect you from the precarious life with which your mother's voice has taken you."

Carla wanted to explain that it was to save them from starvation but all she could think of was that Rákó was leaving her.

Her whole mind and body felt numb from the shock of it.

As the carriage moved on, as if he could not bear to look at her, Rákó returned to the back seat beside her.

But he kept as far away from her as possible.

He stared out of the window, his lips pressed together, his jaw squared, like a man battling with himself.

They drove in silence until, as they neared the Hôtel, Carla said in a voice he could hardly hear:

"Can I . . not see you . . to say . . goodbye?"

"We are saying goodbye now," he answered. "I am staying at the Palace, and the Emperor will understand that I have had to cut my visit short and leave tomorrow."

"You are . . staying . . at the . .Palace?" Carla said in surprise. "I . .never thought . . that was . . where you . .might be."

"Does it matter if I am in a Palace or a hovel if I cannot have you?" Rákó asked.

There was no answer to this.

Then the horses came to a standstill.

Carla realised they had arrived back at the Sacher Hôtel.

They drove up to the front entrance, and now, because it was late, the Journalists and the autograph hunters had gone.

At the same time, Carla was frightened to go in alone in case she encountered the Baron again.

Once more, as he was always able to do, Rákó read her thoughts.

"I will take you up to your Suite," he said.

He helped her out of the carriage, and they walked into the Hall.

"Ask for your key," he suggested.

"The door to our Suite is unlocked," Carla replied.

She remembered that was how she had left it before she went downstairs to where Rákó was waiting for her.

He would never wait for her again.

Step by step, as they walked up the stairs she found herself saying in her heart:

"This is . . the last time . . the last time . . the last time . . ."

There was no one about and only as they reached the landing on which their Suite was situated did she wonder if her mother was back.

As she asked herself the question Rákó answered it for her.

"I think your mother will be very late tonight . ."

Carla opened the door of the Sitting-Room.

Instantly there was the fragrance of the flowers and by the light of a candelabrum which stood on one of the tables she could see the brilliance of them in every corner of the room.

Then she was aware that although she was standing just inside the door Rákó had not followed her.

She turned back and saw him standing at the top of the stairs, a few feet away from her.

She thought as she looked at him that no man could look more handsome, more attractive, or more masculine.

She wanted to throw herself into his arms and beg him not to leave her, but love her just a little longer before they must part.

Then she saw the pain in his eyes and the lines that were suddenly etched on his face told her he was suffering in the same way that she was.

"Goodbye, my lovely one, Heart of my Heart, Light of my Life," he said.

He did not move or make a gesture towards her.

She felt he had enveloped himself in an invisible armour which she could not penetrate.

"G.good . . bye . . ."

She whispered the words.

Her voice broke and she turned away, so that he would not see the tears that had sprung to her eyes.

She went into the Sitting-Room then, and although she did not shut the door behind her she knew he had left.

She stood still for some minutes without seeing the flowers, only feeling their beauty hurting her unbearably.

It was as if they and Rákó had plunged a dagger into her breast and she was bleeding from the agony of it.

Then as her tears threatened to overwhelm her she pushed the Sitting-Room door to without looking out and went into her bedroom.

There was a small candelabrum with three candles burning beside her bed.

She moved unsteadily towards it, wanting to throw herself down and cry despairingly.

Suddenly she became aware of a large, dark object in the corner near the window, and she screamed.

For a moment she did not know who it was, but was just aware that it was another person.

Then when she would have screamed again, her voice died in her throat as she was aware that it was the Baron.

"I have waited a long time for you," he said, "and I should be interested to know where you have been while your mother was disporting herself at the Palace."

"W. what are you . . doing here?" Carla stammered.

"I should have thought that was obvious," he replied.

"You escaped from me once. You will not escape again!"

He came towards her, and now she screamed as she tried to evade him.

Before she could do so, he picked her up and threw her down on the bed.

The violence of it took her by surprise and for a moment she felt stunned.

Then as he flung himself on top of her, she screamed again.

. . . .

Rákó went quickly down the stairs knowing that if he stayed one moment longer he would take Carla into his arms.

The agony of their parting would then be even worse than it was at the moment.

He knew he was crucifying himself in leaving her, and that what he felt was something he would never feel again for any other woman.

At the same time, it had been drummed into him since he was a small boy that he held a unique position.

He was Head of the Rákóczy family, which was admired and respected over the whole of Hungary.

Over and over again he had been told of how his famous ancestor with two of his friends had tried to fight a corrupt and disreputable Monarchy.

He had failed but his dignity and humanity both during his troubles and in exile had never been forgotten.

The Hungarians always believed that had his rebellion succeeded he would have made a very great King.

After his failure, when his great estates were confiscated, his Castle was leased to various nobles of the Imperial Court.

Now the Emperor Franz Joseph allowed Rákó to live there.

Although he had another Castle at Szérencs, he could still feel the vibrations of his great ancestor in the castle which bore his name.

With the help of his family, Rákó had acquired back many of the huge Vineyards from which the Rákóczy family had made their money.

Now through his brilliance he was a very rich man.

He spent his money in building up the family image as it had been in the 15th and 16th centuries.

He wanted to make sure that everything they did was for the glory of Hungary.

He knew in these circumstances it was impossible for him to take a wife of whom his family would be ashamed.

They had already begged him to marry, and he had when he was young, been engaged to be married.

The girl, who had Royal blood in her veins, had died before the wedding could take place.

After that it was easier for him to refuse the ceaseless requests of his relations to start a family of his own.

Yet he was very conscious that one day it was something that he must do.

Then he had seen Carla.

He had known from the moment he set eyes on her that she had already filled the shrine in his heart which until that moment had remained empty.

'I love her! God, how I love her!' he thought despairingly as he reached the bottom of the stairs.

Then as he saw a porter waiting to open the door for him he put his hand in his pocket to find a coin to give him.

Instead he felt the softness of Carla's long, kid glove he had taken from her hand in the carriage.

Because he thought she might miss it, he turned round and went up the stairs.

He thought if the door was still open he would put it just inside the Sitting-Room.

Otherwise he would leave it on the landing and housemaids would think Carla had dropped it when she returned home.

As he reached the landing, he looked down at the glove in his hand and because Carla had worn it he lifted it to his lips.

As he did so, he heard her scream.

. . . .

The Baron was very large and very heavy.

As he lay on top of Carla she felt as if he would crush her.

Although she struggled to push him away from her, she knew it was impossible.

He was trying to kiss her, but she was turning her head from side to side frantically in order to prevent him from doing so.

Then she was aware that he was pulling at the bodice of her gown and she screamed in sheer terror at what he was about to do.

"You are mine!" he said in his thick gutteral voice. "Mine and you cannot escape!"

Even as he said the last word the door into the Sitting-Room burst open.

One glance at the bed told Rákó what was happening.

Before the Baron was aware that he was there, he had seized him by the neck of his coat and pulled him violently off Carla.

Then as the Baron struggled to turn towards him Rákó hit him on the chin, and knocked him to the ground.

Being a big man the Baron fell heavily.

As he started to pour out a stream of loud oaths at his

assailant the light from the candles was on Rákó's furious face.

Suddenly the Baron was silent.

Then in a different voice he exclaimed:

"Your Highness!"

"Get out of here, you swine!" Rákó exclaimed. "How dare you behave in this disgraceful fashion! I shall inform His Majesty of your appalling behaviour!"

Slowly the Baron got to his feet, trying to straighten his evening-coat. Then he said:

"I can explain, Your Highness . . .!"

"Get out!" Rákó repeated. "And if you want satisfaction, I am quite prepared to give it to you!"

"No, no!" the Baron said quickly. "I can only apologise . . ."

Rákó was not listening.

He walked to the bedroom door which led out on to the landing, unlocked it, and held it open.

Shiftily and almost humbly the Baron left. Rákó shut the door and locked it.

Then he turned to look at Carla.

She was sitting up on the bed staring at him, her face was very pale, and there was a stricken expression in her eyes.

"It is all right, my darling," Rákó said. "He will not frighten you again."

It was then Carla put her hands up to her eyes and burst into tears.

Rákó sat down on the bed and pulled her against him

"It is all right," he said soothingly, "you are safe."

"He . . was . . hiding in my . . room," Carla sobbed, "and . . and he . . tried to . . k. kiss me!"

Her words were almost incoherent, but Rákó knew she did not understand exactly what the Baron had intended.

His arms tightened. Then he said:

"It is no use. I cannot allow this to happen because you are so incredibly beautiful."

He kissed her forehead before he said very quietly:

"Will you marry me, my darling, then no other man will ever touch you again!"

Because she was crying Carla did not understand for the moment what he had said.

Then she raised her face to his and he saw her wet eye-lashes and the tears streaming down her cheeks.

"D.did you . . ask me to . . m.marry you?" she whispered.

Rákó pulled her closer to him.

"I am going to marry you!" he said, "and nothing – and I mean nothing – matters except that we should be together."

Then he was kissing her.

Carla felt as if he took her from the depths of Hell up into the sunlit Heavens where the angels were singing.

. . . .

Rákó was still kissing Carla when they heard voices outside on the landing.

Carla made a little exclamation and moved from his arms.

"That will be . . Mama," she said. "I must . . tell her about . . us."

"I will explain," Rákó said.

Carla got off the bed and ran to unlock the door which led into the Sitting-Room.

As she did so her mother came in through the other door looking, Carla thought, not only lovely, but excited.

Her eyes were shining and there was an expression on her face which made her daughter look at her in surprise.

As she moved across the room towards her she was

suddenly aware that the man following her mother was not Mr. Dessoff, as she had expected, but someone else.

"Darling, I am glad you are not asleep!" her mother exclaimed. "I have so much to tell you, and I could not have borne to have waited until the morning."

"And I have . . ." Carla began.

But Lady Milbanke interrupted her, saying:

"First, dearest, I want to introduce you to a very old friend who I never expected to see at the Palace, of all places!"

She turned round and now Carla could see that the man standing behind her was dark, very good-looking.

He was wearing a great number of decorations on his evening-coat.

He was, she thought swiftly, perhaps forty, or a little older.

He was looking at her mother in what she felt was a very intimate manner.

"This, Umberto," Lady Milbanke said to him," is my daughter Carla!"

Carla put out her hand and her mother went on:

"And, dearest, this is the *Duca* Umberto di Valdagno, whom I have known ever since I was a little girl."

"The most beautiful little girl there ever was!" the *Duca* said in English, "and I have loved you, Maria, from the very first time you came to my father's *Palazzo* and tried to catch the gold-fish in the fountain!"

Lady Milbanke laughed.

"I remember those gold-fish and of course I remembered you!"

"And I never forgot you!" the *Duca* said.

There was so much feeling in the way he spoke that Carla could only look from him to her mother in a bewildered fashion.

Lady Milbanke put her hand in hers.

"You may think it very precipitate, my dearest," she

said, "but Umberto has asked me to marry him, and we are leaving for Rome tomorrow!"

Carla gasped as if she could not be hearing aright, and the *Duca* said:

"I think I must explain, Carla, that I have loved your mother all these years, and when she was seventeen I knew she was the only person for me in the whole world, but I was at sea, because I had a Commission in the Italian Navy!"

"And you . . loved Mama!" Carla murmured.

She felt she was being rather stupid, and it was difficult to understand what was happening.

"Yes, I loved her," the *Duca* said, "and when I learnt she had married Lord Milbanke, I knew I had lost the most precious thing in the world!"

"Did you say," a voice questioned behind them, "that Maris Ravello was married to Lord Milbanke?"

Rákó had stood still in the doorway to the bedroom when Carla had run forward to greet her mother.

Now he joined them in the centre of the room and both Lady Milbanke and the *Duca* turned to look at him in surprise.

Then the *Duca* said:

"Good evening, Your Highness! I wondered why you were not at the dinner tonight."

Rákó moved to stand beside Carla as he said to Lady Milbanke:

"I have the honour, *Madame* to ask you for your daughter Carla's hand in marriage!"

Lady Milbanke gave a little cry of amazement. Then she asked:

"But – who are you? And why are you here? I do not understand!"

"Forgive me, Mama," Carla said, "but I have met Rákó since I have been in Vienna . . and we talked . . in the Opera House and now I . . love him!"

Lady Milbanke was still looking bewildered and the *Duca* said:

"Let me explain, Maria. Your daughter wishes to marry a most delightful and talented young man, who is one of the hereditary Princes of Hungary and certainly the most important of them."

"And you wish to marry Carla?" Lady Milbanke asked.

"As soon as it is possible," Rákó answered with a smile.

As he spoke his fingers tightened on Carla's. Then he said:

"I had no idea – you did not tell me – that your father was Lord Milbanke!"

"There were . . so many . . other things to . . talk about," Carla went on and blushed.

"Did you know my husband?" Lady Milbanke asked gently.

"I met him on various occasions," Rákó replied, "and admired him very much."

He drew in his breath and as if a great burden had fallen from his shoulders he said:

"I know my family will welcome the daughter of such a distinguished Diplomat as my wife."

As the *Duca* listened, his eyes were twinkling.

As if he understood exactly what Rákó had been feeling, he said:

"We all have plans to make, and as they are very important, I think we should sit down."

Carla laughed.

"The difficulty is – where?"

She went to the sofa and moved a number of bouquets which had arrived late in the evening, and had not yet been put in water.

Then she cleared two chairs in the same way, and as

her mother she sat down on the sofa, Rákó and the *Duca* occupied the arm-chairs.

"Now let me tell you, Rákó – and I cannot go on calling you Your Highness if you are to be my step-son – what Maria and I have been planning," the *Duca* began.

"I am listening with the greatest attention," Rákó replied, "And I feel it is important to us all."

"It is!" the *Duca* agreed.

He paused for a moment before he said:

"Maria is going to 'disappear' tomorrow, and the Viennese will really believe that she was the '*Spirit of Valhalla*' to where she has now returned!"

"I . . I do not . . understand," Carla said.

"It was a mistake," the *Duca* answered, "as your mother appreciates, for her to have appeared on the stage, even though her voice is the most perfect sound anyone has ever heard."

"The only alternative . . ." Carla began.

The *Duca* held up his hand.

"Your mother had already told me how poor you were, and I swear it is something which will never happen again."

He looked at Lady Milbanke very tenderly and went on:

"But because now, through war, accident or illness, I have become what I never expected to be, head of my family, I have no wish for them to know that your mother has accepted payment for singing in public."

"I . . understand," Carla said in a low voice.

She did not look at Rákó.

But she knew his eyes were on her and she thought how wonderful it had been of him to ask her to be his wife.

He felt as the *Duca* did that it was degrading that

ordinary people should be able to pay to hear a Lady sing.

"I think, if he is honest, Rákó, is up against the same difficulty," the *Duca* said.

"I am ready to marry Carla whatever the difficulties!" Rákó said fiercely, "although I admit they exist."

"That," the *Duca* said dryly, "is why we must eliminate them. "Now, what we are going to do is this . . ."

He bent forward and spoke with an intensity and at the same time, a sense of the dramatic which Carla thought was very Italian.

She knew as he did so that she liked him and that he was exactly the right person to make her mother happy.

It seemed incredible that all this should happen.

Only a short time ago she was striken with fear, and desperate because the Baron was assaulting her.

Rákó had saved her, and she felt her love for him well up in her like the waves of the sea.

She wanted to throw herself into his arms and tell him how much she loved him.

Even as she thought of it, their eyes met, and she knew that he was thinking the same thing.

"What I have planned," the *Duca* was saying, "is quite simple. Maria and I will leave for Rome tomorrow, and we will be married secretly and very quietly as soon as we arrive. Then I will announce to my family that I have a wife who is the widow of the distinguished Lord Milbanke, and I know they will be delighted."

"And Maria Ravello will never sing again!" Lady Milbanke said.

"You will sing for me, my darling," the *Duca* replied, "and just occasionally for our most distinguished friends, or perhaps for one of the many Italian charities which are always desperate for money."

"I want to . . sing for . . you," Lady Milbanke said softly.

"And I want to hear you," the *Duca* replied.

They were speaking to each other as if they were alone.

Then with an effort he said:

"I suggest, Rákó, that you do the same thing, and take Carla to Hungary to meet your family."

He paused a moment before he went on:

"I feel sure when it is announced that you have married the daughter of the late and very distinguished Lord Milbanke and the *Duchessa* Umberto di Valdagno, you will receive many congratulations."

The eyes of the two men met.

Carla was intelligent enough to know that however much Rákó loved her, he was relieved that there would be no unpleasantness over her antecedents.

"I shall try to see you after our marriage, darling," Lady Milbanke said to Carla.

"I have thought of that," the *Duca* interposed, "and as I am taking you on a long honeymoon I think perhaps on our way back to Rome we might be invited to Castle Rákóczi."

Rákó spread out his hands.

"All I have is yours!"

They all laughed at the age-old saying.

Then Carla exclaimed:

"It all sounds very wonderful, but I cannot help feeling rather sorry for Mr. Dessoff. He has been so kind, and he had also spent a great deal of . . money on . . us."

"It will be returned to him," the *Duca* said. "At the same time, he is going to be a very happy man, even though he has lost his *Prima Donna* with the voice of an angel."

"Why is he going to be happy?" Carla enquired.

"Because the Emperor told me tonight before dinner," the *Duca* explained, "that he intends to give

Mr. Dessoff the greatest accolade that can be paid to anyone connected with music."

"And what is that?" Carla asked.

"Both Johann Strauss and Gustav Dessoff are to be given the Freedom of the City of Vienna, which is of course, the City of Love!"

Carla clasped her hands together.

"Did the Emperor really say that? How wonderful! I know how thrilled and happy Mr. Dessoff will be."

"And so will Johann Strauss," the *Duca* smiled.

"Now that is settled," Carla said, "there is one question I must ask"

"What is that?" her mother enquired.

"Who, Mama, gave you that wonderful necklace?"

Lady Milbanke smiled.

"I thought you might have guessed the answer."

"You mean . . it was the *Duca*?"

"When I heard the night before last that we were to attend the Opening night of '*Die Walküre*'," the *Duca* said, "I was not particularly interested, as I find Wagner's music rather over-powering."

The three people he was talking to were all listening as he went on:

"Then, when we entered the Royal Box and I looked at the programme I saw to my astonishment the name Maria Ravello!"

"Did you know it was me?" Lady Milbanke enquired.

"I thought it could not possibly be, and that somebody had merely used your name," the *Duca* replied.

He looked at her very lovingly before he went on:

"Then when you came on the stage and I heard the first notes of your voice I knew it was you!"

He drew in his breath.

"How could you have hidden yourself away all these years so that you were never where I expected to find you? Yet, in a way – you were always with me."

"Oh, Umberto, did you really feel like that?" Lady Milbanke asked. "It seems strange, yet because you were at sea, and we were travelling from country to country, we never met."

"I not only remembered the most beautiful little girl I have ever known," the *Duca* said, "but I also remembered her voice."

"If Papa had not married Mama, would you have asked her to be your wife?" Carla asked.

She felt the story was so fantastic that she had to know the details.

"It was what I wanted," the *Duca* said simply, "but I had nothing to offer someone as beautiful as your mother. I was an Officer in a battleship with no expectation of being anything but a poor man for the rest of my life."

"But now, everything has changed!" Carla said excitedly, "and you are very important, and very rich!"

"Really, darling!" Lady Milbanke admonished.

"It is true," the *Duca* answered, "and as I say, quite by chance, and with fate working towards our happiness, I am, as Carla says 'very important and very rich!' "

He laughed as if he thought he should not boast.

It flashed through Carla's mind how very different he was from the Baron, who had tried to impress her with his social importance and his wealth.

Then she told herself she need never think of that man again.

Rákó had punished him so effectively that he would always be afraid of what he migh say about him.

"And now we have nothing to do except to pack," Lady Milbanke said, "and of course be happier than we have ever been in our lives before."

As she spoke she thought she had been too impulsive and putting her hand out to her daughter, she cried:

"You do understand, darling, that I loved your father

and he was very kind to me, but Umberto, although I suppose I should not say it, has always had a place in my heart."

"I do understand, Mama," Carla said, "and I am so very, very grateful that my prayers and the candles I lit in the Stephansdom have brought us everything I asked for, only it is very much more wonderful!"

She looked at Rákó as she spoke and saw a little flash of fire in his eyes.

Lady Milbanke put her hand up to her neck.

"You were telling Carla," she said to the *Duca* "about my necklace. it was such a surprise and I could not imagine who could have given me anything so beautiful!"

"When I realised that the '*Spirit of Valhalla*' was *my* Maria," the *Duca* said, "I wanted to sweep you off the stage in my arms and take you away so that nobody else should ever look at you again!"

Carla saw her mother quiver at the *Duca's* words before he went on:

"It was impossible for me to leave the Emperor all day yesterday when he had arranged for me to inspect his troops outside Vienna, and we left the Palace early in the morning."

He paused before he went on:

"When we returned, it was too late to get in touch with you because you would have been at the Opera House."

Lady Milbanke was stroking her necklace as he talked, but her eyes were on his face.

"Then this morning," he said, "I managed to slip away from the Palace, and the moment I saw the necklace in a Jeweller's shop I knew that the right place for it was around your lovely neck."

"Mama was waiting to find out who had given it to her so that she could thank them, but give it back,"

Carla said, "because she felt it was something she could not accept."

"You certainly would not have been allowed to accept it from anyone but me!" the *Duca* said to Lady Milbanke, "but it is the first of many things I intend to give you."

"And . . what can . . I give . . you?" Lady Milbanke asked.

"Yourself, my darling, and your exquisite voice," the *Duca* answered. "Both those things are for me, and me alone, and I promise you I shall make certain of that!"

Carla knew that Rákó was thinking the same thing, and as the *Duca* and her mother rose to their feet, she slipped her hand into his.

The touch of him told her without words how much he would protect her and look after her.

Now the future would be very different from the anxiety, the problems and the fear she had experienced in the past.

"There is something I want to show you," Rákó said.

He took her across the room and out through the door on to the landing.

When they got there he pointed to her glove which he had thrown on the carpet when he had heard her scream and said:

"That is what brought me back."

"Oh, Rákó, supposing . . you had not . . come? Suppose . . .?"

"Forget him!" Rákó interrupted.

He put his arms around Carla and held her close against him.

"Nothing like that shall ever happen to you again, my darling!" he vowed. "You are mine and I will look after you and be a very, very, jealous husband!"

"That . . is what I . . want you . . to be," Carla whispered.

"It is what I will be!" he replied.

His lips were very near to hers as he said:

"We will be married as soon as we reach my Castle. I dare not wait in case you disappear and I find this has all been a dream!"

"That is what . . I have been . . thinking," Carla said. "But it is true . . Oh, Rákó . . tell me it . . is true!"

"It is true, my beautiful darling!" he replied, "and I knew, even while I tried to do what I thought was right, I could never have let you go!"

"You came . . back!" she said. "You came . . back just . . because of my . . glove!"

"If it had not been that excuse, it would have been another," Rákó said. "We are part of each other, Carla, and it is impossible for me to tell you how much I love you!"

"As I . . love you," Carla whispered. "You fill my whole world, and like Mama's voice, you carry me up . . into the . . sky."

"The music of love will be with us all our lives," Rákó said, "and I promise you, my darling, that our happiness will radiate out over everybody who knows us, and also over my beloved Hungary."

"Only you could say anything so wonderful!" Carla said. "Oh, Rákó, love me . . please love me . . because without your love . . I can no longer go on . . living.'

Rákó did not answer.

His lips found hers and he was kissing her not gently, but demandingly, passionately and possessively.

She was his, completely, and nothing could ever separate them again.

They were one person; one in a Divine Light which, like the music of love, is part of God.

ABOUT THE AUTHOR

Barbara Cartland, the world's most famous romantic novelist, who is also an historian, playwright, lecturer, political speaker and television personality, has now written over 490 books and sold nearly 500 million copies all over the world.

She has also had many historical works published and has written four autobiographies as well as the biographies of her mother and that of her brother, Ronald Cartland, who was the first Member of Parliament to be killed in the last war. This book has a preface by Sir Winston Churchill and has just been republished with an introduction by the late Sir Arthur Bryant.

"Love at the Helm" a novel written with the help and inspiration of the late Earl Mountbatten of Burma, Great Uncle of His Royal Highness The Prince of Wales, is being sold for the Mountbatten Memorial Trust.

She has broken the world record for the last thirteen years by writing an average of twenty-three books a year. In the Guinness Book of Records she is listed as the world's top-selling author.

Miss Cartland in 1978 sang an Album of Love Songs with the Royal Philharmonic orchestra.

In private life Barbara Cartland, who is a Dame of Grace of the Order of St. John of Jerusalem, Chairman of the St. John Council in Hertfordshire and Deputy President of the St. John Ambulance Brigade, has fought for better conditions and salaries for Midwives and Nurses.

She championed the cause for the Elderly in 1956 invoking a Government Enquiry into the "Housing Conditions of Old People".

In 1962 she had the Law of England changed so that Local Authorities had to provide camps for their own Gypsies. This has meant that since then thousands and thousands of Gypsy children have been able to go to School which they had never been able to do in the past, as their caravans were moved every twenty-four hours by the Police.

There are now fourteen camps in Hertfordshire and Barbara Cartland has her own Romany Gypsy Camp called Barbaraville by the Gypsies.

Her designs "Decorating with Love" are being sold all over the U.S.A. and the National Home Fashions League made her, in 1981, "Woman of Achievement".

Barbara Cartland's book "Getting Older, Growing Younger" has been published in Great Britain and the U.S.A. and her fifth Cookery Book, "The Romance of Food", is now being used by the House of Commons.

In 1984 she received at Kennedy Airport, America's Bishop Wright Air Industry Award for her contribution to the development of aviation. In 1931 she and two R.A.F. Officers thought of, and carried the first aeroplane-towed glider air-mail.

During the War she was Chief Lady Welfare Officer in Bedfordshire looking after 20,000 Service men and women. She thought of having a pool of Wedding Dresses at the War Office so a Service Bride could hire a gown for the day.

She bought 1,000 gowns without coupons for the A.T.S., the W.A.A.F.s and the W.R.E.N.S. In 1945 Barbara Cartland received the Certificate of Merit from Eastern Command.

In 1964 Barbara Cartland founded the National Association for Health of which she is the President, as a front for all the Health Stores and for any product made as an alternative medicine.

This has now a £500,000,000 turnover a year, with one third going in export.

In January 1988 she received "La Medaille de Vermeil de la Ville de Paris", (the Gold Medal of Paris). This is the highest award to be given by the City of Paris for ACHIEVEMENT – 25 million books sold in France.

In March 1988 Barbara Cartland was asked by the Indian Government to open their Health Resort outside Delhi. This is almost the largest Health Resort in the World.

Barbara Cartland was received with great enthusiasm by her fans, who also fêted her at a Reception in the city and she received the gift of an embossed plate from the Government.